Blow Your Nose in Dirty Clothes:
A Man's Guide to Practices in Frugality

by

Michael O'Neal

RoseDog Books
PITTSBURGH, PENNSYLVANIA 15238

RoseDog Books
585 Alpha Drive, Suite 103
Pittsburgh, PA 15238
Visit our website at *www.rosedogbookstore.com*

ISBN: 979-8-88812-098-9
eISBN: 979-8-88812-598-4

Dedication

To my grandparents and parents. I will be forever grateful for their role-modeling, training, and sound advice on saving money, working hard, and appreciating where I was at each turn in my life.

And to Lisha. We share the same page.

Other Books by Michael O'Neal

Travel Stories

Being in Beijing: Buses, Bikes, and Beer

Stuck in the Sharjah Sandbox

Charmed in Chengdu

Fiction

Of All the Animals

Introduction

My Great Uncle Bob, a successful, and *honest,* used car salesmen, taught me at an early age to walk with my eyes to the ground, semi-good advice for a clumsy kid. I didn't trip as much with my eyes glued to the few inches of dirt or walkway in front of me, but I did bang my noggin on things just beyond the distance of my toes. My dad would shake his head when I'd amble into low-hanging branches, parking meters, other people, and store front doors, calling out, "Stumblebum!" Or he'd need grab me by the neck when I'd unwittingly walk into oncoming traffic, scolding me, "Watch where the hell you're going, Knucklehead!" Why the sage advice from Uncle Bob? For finding fumbled coins, of course.

My Grandfather and his brother, Robert (Uncle Bob), were born at end of the 19th century. When the Great Depression hit in 1929, they were family men in their early 30's. Frugality was a necessity, not a lifestyle choice. Those times were hard enough that many were tempted to, and did, commit lesser crimes. Pocketing an apple from the vendors' stand, quickly snagging and arm-tucking a newspaper left unattended or sliding a coffee mug from a busy diner counter into a purse.

Along with the depression was prohibition. My grandfather brewed basement beer in a clawfoot tub, another of his brothers, George, was more the traditional 1920's gangster, a bootlegger. Uncle George went to prison. He held the record for solitary confinement—a hole in the ground—after he beat up a screw (guard) and wouldn't apologize*. My Grampa confessed to stealing coal during those days, but didn't get caught, didn't serve time.

As my grampa related, "We'd just moved to the town of Yankton, South Dakota. My neighbors got mad at me when they saw I'd bought a sack of heating coal. 'You don't buy coal', they told me. 'It'll make the coal delivery guys wonder why the rest of us aren't buyin' coal, and that could be trouble. You take a gunny sack, go down along the tracks and collect what's fallen off the coal cars."' As kid-innocent-ethical as I was, even I didn't consider that stealing. It was like finding change on the ground, finders' keepers, and all that.

Pinching pennies and looking for dropped coinage quickly became a practice for me, bolstered by the superstition of finding that all-day-long, good luck copperhead. To this day I cannot walk over a pavement penny without bending to pick it up. And my grandfather added to my hope for acquiring more money by telling me to keep the green side of dollar bills face-up in my Roy Rogers wallet.

*During shower time, the guard told Uncle George to remove his Black Hills gold ring. No way. He'd never see it again. The guard pulled his night stick. Uncle George commandeered the night stick and wrapped it around the guard's neck. Solitaire. How unfair. Uncle George finally got out of the hole when the prison got a new warden. The ring is worn thin, missing a stone, is bent, beautiful, and rests in my safe.

"Why, Grampa?"
"Like grass, green grows."
Ah, the Irish. I'm now in my 60's, can't break either habit. As foolish as I sometimes feel from the training, I still check vending machine change slots, (I miss pay phones), and ogle casino carpeting more than the low, neck lines of the buxom cocktail servers. But I've picked up lots of paper money besides coins, my buddies and others having stepped over or on top of $5 bills. You can't tell me it's not thrilling to look down and find a $20. My record find was a $100 bill on a sidewalk in San Antonio that two of my friends walked over and my son stepped on. I bought the next two rounds of beers along the River Walk.

If you have plenty of money and have no need to keep tabs on your spending, or you have no desire to conserve or recycle for the care of the planet, or you do not care about teaching your children the importance of conservation, a good work ethic, and good values, or if you are narcissistic and/or spoiled, then read no further.

Otherwise, read on, Buddy. But be prepared to be scolded, offended, grossed out, or think me foolish. Enh, you're men. You can handle it.

If, on the other hand—and this must be so because you continue reading this intro—you want to save up to thousands of dollars a year, raise children who respect you and the value of work and assume responsibility, and do your part in not being part of such an extremely wasteful society, American or otherwise, read away!

Get away from living paycheck to paycheck. Have extra money for some fun in life. Payoff your mortgage and your credit cards. Travel, be debt free, build a nest egg, create a legacy for your children to pass on. If you are of an age to complain about the lacking character of millennials, well Christ, you created them!

We might even get to a point where the United States of America functions better, both socially and financially. The blame for the crash in 2008 could be viably widespread, not only the fault of those unscrupulous lenders and NRON. On Oct. 11, 2013, we were into our second week of a government shutdown! As if we needed air traffic controllers.

And now, in 2022, we face unprecedented inflation and relatively exorbitant prices from gas to large eggs and lumber to chicken legs.

But above all, have fun with my suggestions. Maybe rethink a few of your current wasteful and spendthrift habits.

Part 1: Dads, Dinners, and Dating

Chapter 1: FOOD

Each American, on average (2018), wastes about one pound of food each day, far surpassing the 38 million tons tossed in 2014. Having worked lunch duty in several secondary schools I'm surprised those numbers aren't higher. A not-so-small country could feed its entire population for a year on the perfectly good and expensive food we so casually toss into trash cans or leave on our plates uneaten each day.

A 12-year-old boy approached me in tears during lunch one day at one of the junior high schools where I loved teaching. I thought he had been picked on, my hackles snapping to attention. 'John' was recently from Uganda, and was one of the nicest, most polite and respectful kids I'd ever encountered, and I'd been teaching for twenty-plus years at that point.

"Sir, the students throw away their food!"

I cocked my head, my hand on his thin shoulder.

"There is more in one trash can than to feed my village for two days!", he cried, his small fists clenched at his sides. I put my arm around him, patting his diminutive back. There was no defense for what his US classmates were guilty of.

The USA is a great country, but we've moved well beyond the 1950's when production and consumption, as well as a growing population, were grounds for boasting. We've come to realize that bigger is not necessarily better in terms of Climate Change, Carbon Foot-printing, and the Polluting of Our Planet. James Loewen stated that "Each American born in the 1970's will generate 126 tons of garbage (lots being food waste) and 9.8 tons of particulate air pollution." Jared Diamond estimated that in 2005, "...the average American consumed thirty-two times as much of the world's largesse and produced thirty-two times as much pollution as the average Third World citizen." It's a no-brainer in assuming wealth and consumption may create comfort, but that does not necessarily equate to happiness, good health, or conscientious stewardship.

Over the past fifty years, Americans increasingly see themselves as less happy than each preceding decade. My secondary teaching credential was for Social Studies. I primarily taught American and World History. From 1984 to 2013, once a year, I asked each of my classes if they saw the world becoming a better place in the next 100 years, or would things get worse. Few students had the more positive outlook, maybe 20%. The reasons for the bleaker predictions had less to do with warfare than it did with the poisoning our air and water, abuses with food production (pesticides) and consumption (waste and starvation), and fears of getting cancer. Two young students had cancers one school year, one of them died.

Food collections for the needy was an annual activity, despite the neighborhood that was largely middle-class. Ironic that for the past several years, if not decades, enough food is produced worldwide to feed EVERYONE on this swirling rock!

In July 2000, I experienced Kenya, thirty other adults in the group, most of them teachers. What a beautiful and hospitable country, finely tuned with catering to tourist, their number one industry. Kenya was in the middle of a continuing drought that year. But that did not keep an abundance of food from being spread out for us on long tables, bottled drinking water a slight reach away. After a lunch of pasta, seasoned rice, spiced lamb (maybe goat), sauced lentils, and fresh fruits, served out in the open on the Serengeti, I stepped away to take a leak in the brush, hoping I wouldn't piss-off— or on—a cobra. When I returned to the tables, the group was leaving, shuffling from the tables to begin re-boarding the vans. Waiters were clearing away the dirty dishes and bowls of half-eaten food. I couldn't help but notice them, words unspoken, holding up half empty bottles of water and unfinished plates of food, their facial expressions and shakes of their heads showing a reserved look of, "Americans..., they have no idea." I was immediately embarrassed and ashamed.

The people I was traveling with were good folk, fun to be with, educated. They were also, ultimately, totally unaware of their surroundings and how offensively ethnocentric and elitist they'd just shown themselves. I put my hand over my heart, mouthing an apology to the men. They smiled and waved me off, "Hakuna matata." They were far too forgiving. I wouldn't have blamed them for voicing a curse or two.

Just a couple of days later we'd ridden camels across the plain to a noted waterfall. It dumped over the cliffside resembling the flush of a toilet; sudsy, shit-brown, and without much force due to the drought. We had climbed up the opposing cliff bank, viewing the falls from above. We were served box lunches. The same thing happened. My travel mates left untouched fruit, bottles of water, and wrapped sandwiches to be thrown away. Nope, not on my watch.

I went to almost every person gathering up their uneaten food and still sealed waters. I whistled down to our camel wranglers and began making a game of tossing down the leftovers. Not one man missed a single throw of apple, orange, pickle, or bottle of water.

"Hey, Mike." It was our guide, Cosmo, who had quietly summoned me. He pulled me aside. "I saw what you did." He shook my hand, nodding his head, looking me directly in the eye. "No one ever does that."

I've traveled to over fifty countries, never witnessing the waste of food I've seen in the US. Even some of the homeless here need not worry about starving, and I admire their scavenging cleverness. They even tend to be chubby. They raid the dumpsters behind expensive restaurants, selecting day-old sour dough bread, partially eaten but relatively untainted prime rib and T-bone steaks, whole untouched halves of an assortment of sandwiches, and all else waved away by hoity-toity patrons. Smarter—or lazier—bums hang out in front of these restaurants seated on nearby park benches, hands held out for the leftovers carried in Styrofoam or cardboard containers. (I suppose that food wouldn't be counted as waste, but as a donation).

Anyway, food for thought, here is a cornucopia of ways to not waste food.

A. Expiration Dates: Groceries do not go 'bad' on the 'best if sold by' date, or that soon after the expiration date. If the food doesn't stink, hasn't grown hair or changed much in color or consistency, and if it doesn't move with new life, you are most likely good to go. Even if that cheese reaches an age of growing hair or becomes spotty with mold, or that apple gets a soft spot or has a bruise, these gag-reflexive parts can be peeled off, cut out, boiled away or even washed clean. "Honey, the cheese has hair on it! Where are you going?"

"To get my razor."

If you do get sick because of bacteria you haven't yet built up the enzymes to fight, you'll miss the next few meals, unable to eat, saving even more money on groceries for the next two to three days. And if thinning up is a goal of yours, think of the weight loss.

"Betty, you look so good! Have you lost weight?"

"Yes, Wilma. I ate some fish that had been in the fridge for a bit too long. I got pretty sick, but I lost seven pounds!"

"Good for you! What kind of fish was it and how many days had it been left forgotten? Fred is getting amply plump and I'm at my wits end with ways to get him to trim up."

There are stores nowadays that will purchase 'expired' stocked items in other grocery stores to resell at discounted prices in their stores. This is perfectly legal, ethical, 'Green', and cost effective for both the business and the consumer. It makes me glad that homeless shelters and other agencies come and collect day-old breads and muffins from bakeries, Costco, and other food outlets for dispersing the next day to those in need.

Refrigeration is an amazing advancement for the preservation of food. Meats, dairy, salads, everything lasting much longer when chilled, way past what many people have been falsely led—to the point of paranoia—to be deemed unsafe for consumption. Just because something has been in the fridge for a few days doesn't make it bad. I've lost count of the times I've heard people exclaim, "Oh, that's been in the fridge for a week!"

"So what?"

 "Well, we need to throw it out."

"Because 5-7 days has become the automatic scientific deadline for some reason? Oh, my gawd, a week! You probably need a new fridge as well?"

I remember as a kid, watching a news report on a war-torn area in the Mideast, plenty of displaced and wounded people. The film clip showed a man sitting on the dirty floor of a dirty hospital, awaiting care. He was licking a finger, dabbing it on pieces of gawd-knows-what on the floor, putting those specs of whatever into his mouth. I hoped it was grains of rice as opposed to ants. That three-second scene became a watershed moment for me.

"Mike, that's not the same potato salad that was served at the school bar-be-cue, is it?"

I was walking through the Home Economics teacher's room on my way back to my classroom with a big bowl of the spud salad. Sarah was one of the few teachers I got along with. "Yea, why?"

"It's over two weeks old!"

"So? It's delicious." I tucked a big spoonful into my mouth.

"That is so gross!"

"What? It's not green or furry and the mayonnaise is only just beginning to go clear." Granted, Sarah stopped giving me hugs in greeting from that point on.

Our digestive enzymes can handle quite a bit if they are trained to do so. Of course, I grew up during the decades before anyone had ever heard of gluten, or celiac disease, and food allergies. Bad carbs were dirty or malfunctioning parts in cars, and anorexia was limited to Twiggy and Karen Carpenter. Peanut allergies, serious stuff. But our 1960's Mom's would've raised holy hell if not allowed to bake the cupcakes and brownies for our classrooms. Store-bought!? Blasphemy! A communist plot! Moms sending their kids to school with thirty Hostess Cupcakes would've been expensive and that mom would likely have been reported to CPS! (Oh, not yet. Child Protective Services wasn't really around until 1974. It was only after 1973 that children began to be abused). Moms sending store-bought goodies to school would have simply been shamed out of town. And I think children listened more to their parents back then. Like my friend's mom who reminded him before our walk to school one day:

"Honey, you have a bad allergy to nuts, so don't eat the cupcakes Scott brings to class, even if the lying little turd tells you they're nut-free." Under her breath, "His father should be nut-free." I didn't know what that meant, but I giggled anyway.

Milk easily lasts a week beyond the sell-by date, probably one of the most thrown out, dumped out grocery items. I worked two years teaching at a mental hospital. Lunches were provided, extra lunches and milk stored in a big refrigerator. I was going to pass out some leftover small cartons of milk one day. The secretary almost gouged my neck with a pencil. "Mike, those milks have a passed expiration date!" *People just freak.*

"No, it's the best if sold by date, and that's today."

"Well, it's still bad!"

I opened one up and chugged it. She ran gagging from the room. I laughed so hard I snorted half a mouthful. I brought several cartons home and drank them over the next week and half. Lisha, my equally frugal GF, and I just finished off a jug of milk that had a best-if-sold-by-date of 11/4. Today is the 18th. Use your head, use your nose, sip and evaluate.

My retirement job has been working in the dry foods section at Costco. A man from a foreign land could not find the expiration date on the honey. Holding up the two-pound jug, he asked, "Sir, when does this expire? There is no expiration date on the label."

"It doesn't spoil. Its honey." Honey does not rot; has something to do with the 17% water thing. At 63, I figured everyone had heard the story of archeologists unearthing ancient unspoiled honey in an

Egyptian tomb. *Wouldn't that have been cool?   Heating up and dribbling 3,000-year-old honey onto an English muffin!*

"Mmm, this is good honey. Who made it?"

"Tutankhamun. No big."

The man asked again, "Yes, but how long will last?"

"Longer than you. It's honey. Doesn't spoil. If it crystallizes, just melt it."

"So, it last one month?"

I'd been a teacher for thirty-plus years for students as young as ten, as old as twenty-one, but I was losing patience. I picked up a bottle of expensive Manuka honey. "Pal, if you want honey that last a long time, this is it. Only fifty bucks. All of these other honeys may last forever, but this Manuka stuff, it lasts forever and a day."

 The goof bought the Manuka. And I'd thought sales wasn't my strong point.

Another concern of shoppers is buying more than they can use before the food item goes bad even if at considerable savings. Those eight cans of refired beans can be stacked and stowed. What, people don't have freezers and pantries or garages? Or they forget they do? If you have a freezer, bread freezes just fine, as does milk.

Let me reiterate: Let your nose and eyes be your guides. No need to even check expiration' dates. Dull sense of smell? Fine, borrow a friends' or family members' nose.

B. Cook Quantity: Leftovers mean less energy for cooking as reheating is much quicker, and many leftover dinners can be altered with onions or hamburger or peppers or canned soups in creating new meals. Leftover baked chicken can be stir-fried or made into sandwiches the next day, vegetables and/or beans can be added to a stew*, hamburgers and meat loafs can be broken up and turned into tacos, burritos, or tostadas.

*The fire was never out from under the pots of many Native American tribes—South and North. As roots, herbs and game were gathered or darted, it was cut up and added to the cauldron. Right, bacteria.... Lewis nor Clark ever mentioned any "Indians", Mandan, Sioux, Shoshone, or Duamish, ever getting sick from their own cooking, nor did the men making up The Corps of Discovery. Granted, when the boys of the Corps of Discovery, due to hunger, ate too much camas root, proffered by Sacajawea, they paid for it as depicted in journal entries. "The sweet taste of the root like pumpkin", belied its fibrous effect. "Nearly all the men sick", with gut wrenching painful gas! Not so funny unless in a fart-lighting contest in an open-windowed dorm room. Not that I would know.

My children nicknamed my concoctions, "prison stew". But at the end of the week, so many new food items had been added, it was at least a *different* prison stew daily. And if children are hungry enough, they'll eat what you serve. Not that I ever starved my kids!

"But we hate leftovers."

Here's a good answer to that. "Too bad. How many thousands of Third World kids would cry at what you carelessly throw away because you don't like the idea of leftovers?" *Whiners.*

Some of my favorite after-holiday concoctions are the different soups I get from boiling the carcass of the turkey. I'll end up with a few Tupperware containers of the broth and meat I can pull from the freezer. With an assortment of vegetables added the soups make for hearty, healthy, comfort food meals throughout the winter.

And when you use the oven in the winter, once your food is baked, leave the oven door propped open in the broiler position so the residual heat exhausts into the room. This is also a good way for young children and curious pets to learn caution. *Don't childproof your house. House-proof your child.*

If you are going to put in the time to make a quiche, a nut or fruit bread, cookies, or any other baked item, why not double or triple the recipe? And yes, freeze the extra. Or maybe be a good neighbor and hand off some of the surplus? Lisha and I have spare brownies, banana breads, cookies, and homemade spaghetti sauce in our freezer for quick thaws when the quick and convenient want arises. And when I need my chainsaw sharpened, a proffered dozen cookies ensures that my neighbor, Tim, will gladly break out his file and do the job. If I wait and watch, I sometimes also get a beer out of the deal.

C. Order Less: When out with friends, finish what they don't. I suppose they'd need to be good friends, but whatever. A group of close friends with whom I used to backpack and camp were great to dine with when we'd hit restaurants after our outings. There could be as many as seven or eight of us together at a time, and when we'd barge into a diner, I could bank on having a great dinner—or should I say, dinners. I knew my wife at the time would not finish whatever she'd order, and she never worried about it going to waste since I was there to do the clean up. Two other women in the group were light eaters as well. And the guys, eyes bigger than their stomachs, could also order too much.

"Mike, it that all you're getting; soup?"

My appetite was notorious, and my friends also knew of my obnoxious frugality. My buddy Robert would remind them, "He's banking on some of us not finishing our meals, and we'll pass them over."

"Well, at least nothing will go to waste." I appreciated Robert's wife, Elizabeth, backing me. My dinner would oft times end up consisting of ample portions of beef, chicken, pastas, fish, pork, baked potatoes with the skins, sauteed vegetables, and garlic bread. At the end of many of those meals with friends I'd sometimes have three and four Mike-finished-plates stacked in front of me. I've appreciated my metabolism since youth. I only passed on desserts, not wanting to make a pig of myself—or pay for it. I was almost embarrassed eating the most and paying the least. Almost.

Also, take advantage of two-fers, coupons, unlimited fries, free soda refills and offers like that. My restaurant choices were, for years, determined by the coupons I had collected. TGI Fridays, back in 1982 when I was in college, refilled sodas for free; nice of a bar to do that. I loved my beer, but free soft drinks beat out a $5 IPA. My roommate John C. and I would order deep fried appetizers and suck down 7-

Ups. Incredibly, we still got contact tipsy, and it was lots of fun watching drunk Cal State, Fresno co-eds make complete asses of themselves while we remained sober.

D. Cheap Wines: There are plenty of good wines out there for under $10, even under $5. Gamble, taste and serve. If your guests are of a pickier snobbish pallet, serve your better wines first, the cheaper wines to follow. After three glasses, or even two for light weights, who cares or notices bouquet and body at that point anyway? And if they are considerate guests, they'd bring a bottle.

Don't be shy.

"Mike, what can we bring?"

"Wine!" I serve theirs first—the better stuff—my cheaper stuff, third.

To prove their unwarranted snobbery, tout the cheap wine as a great find from whatever obscure winery of the label, have your guests taste it and then have them guess what you paid. There has never been a time where my guests guessed the proffered swill as ultimately cheap, even with knowing me.

I happened upon a wine at Costco not long ago, only sold by the case. I checked the price and did the math in my head. Wow! I quickly replaced my first-choice cheap wine selections, gambling on this new economical find. Before offering it to my friends, I did sample it, tentatively, half expecting a salad vinegar flavor. It wasn't bad.

I did the touting thing at my next gathering, had my friends take their first sip to approving nods and then had them guess the price. Not so much due to the taste as to my friends knowing of my frugality, I did not get guesses of over $14 a bottle, but still, the average estimate came in at $12. Actual cost: less than $2.50 per bottle. Ha, the human psyche is easily manipulated.

An experiment was done among Sommeliers some time ago to gauge the trump of sight over other senses, like taste. White wine was turned red with food coloring, then offered up to the pros with their trained noses and tongues. There is a vernacular used for wines, depending on its color. Not only did none of the renowned tasters identify the disguised white wine as white they all spoke in terms of the whites as being 'robust red'. Well, well, aren't we haughty? The Sommeliers were not happy about being duped.   Serves their arrogant noses right.

Beyond price, here's a good rule of thumb for wines: If you like it, buy it. Or, cut out drinking all together and save a butt-load of dough. *Right, like that's possible.*

E. Don't Be Lazy: This has much to do with grocery purchases. Consumers pay through the nose when buying prepared foods or prepackaged snacks. You are fully capable, and really do have the time, to do the cutting, prepping, and cooking, bagging, freezing, and planning of boxed lunches, dinners, and snacks. And doing this with your children and/or significant other while sipping cheap red wine can make for good conversation, reconnecting with loved ones, enjoyable one-on-one exchanges, more satisfying family time and romantic meals.

Chop up the lettuce for salads, peel and cut whole carrots, dice and slice whole onions, mushrooms, tomatoes and peppers. Make your own spaghetti sauces, cut up fryer chickens, sometimes (2018) 79 cents/lb., make your own stews and soups from leftovers—new meals from old ones—and grate or slice the cheese yourself. Put on music while doing this. Hopefully, you have a window to gaze out of every few seconds, taking in the beauty of the day, checking on your kids who should be playing in the yard, getting thoroughly dirty and wonderfully wounded. Two days ago, I looked up in time to see a bobcat hurry across my driveway! Deer are a common sight as well as are the big piliated woodpeckers, fluffy-tailed gray squirrels, and chirping chip monks. I would never opt to live in a close neighborhood.

Buying in bulk is less expensive than individual serving sized packaged goods, like cereals and lunch items for kids, and one helluva lot more environmentally friendly. I'm amazed how packaging many times outweighs the food. I once saw for sale a cardboard box, labeled 'toast'. Are you friggin' kidding me? So, to heat it up you put in the toaster?

By involving your children in food prep, you are teaching them self-reliance, the budgeting of money as well as of time, culinary skills, and the in jeopardy, or soon-to-be lost, skill of oral communication. Do not allow cell phones within reach while cooking. In fact, turn them off! Texting should not be allowed from say, 5:00-Bedtime. Your kids will see their friends tomorrow at school. The same goes for you, Pop. Really, how many emergency calls do you take hourly, monthly, or even yearly if ever at all? Forgetting something at home rarely constitutes an emergency, no need for a call. If it had been that important, it wouldn't have been forgotten. You can do without. Another rule for me: I don't turn the car around for a forgotten item; don't want to waste the gas. I know I'll survive the day without my coat, the random list, my lunch box, or even my wallet. After all, how many times a year do I get pulled over by police? Seven? And one day without the flute for my daughter, Kelsey, didn't diminish her chances with playing for the Philharmonic. She was pissed at me, but never again forgot her flute. Yes, I can be a meanie.

Back on track....

Time is something you make time for.

The TV does not need to be on 24/7. You can give Facebook and texting a rest, and porn exposes your computer to viruses and the type of 'pop ups' you don't want to pop up. (Or maybe you do?) Americans are addicted to too many totally unnecessary things that are ultimately time consuming, expensive, and an abusive waste of time. Cook together or for yourself, talk in person to your family, use your time wisely and for good purpose. Read a book? And maybe even be a more productive family member in terms of your family!

Sorry. Scolding again. Having taught junior high school for many years I saw the results of neglected children.

Another way to involve the kids with cooking is not using a blender. There was a time, worldwide, when there was no electricity in homes. People cut, mixed, drilled, sawed, and stirred by hand with the tools and utensils at hand. Without a mixer, the kids and I made great oatmeal chocolate chip cookies. Yes, folding the Crisco into the flour and then mixing that with several cups of oats was a workout. Kelsey and Jake would sit on top of the kitchen island holding the big bowl between them. I foolishly used a long wooden spoon to do the stirring.

"Dad, the spoon's gonna break again", Kelsey would warn.

"Nah, not this time. This one has a thicker handle."

SNAP! *But the broken spoon became kindling.* And Kelsey and Jake realized early on that I was a goof.

Years later I still don't own a fancy expensive mixer, but I have been taught a different stirring technique: chopsticks. "Honey, this is how we always cook. We never had a mixer or blender. And our invention of chopsticks works for many things."

Lisha whorls two chopsticks like a Ninja twirling a nun chuck. No combination of ingredients can thwart her. I purposely dumped all the flour into a mix at once, the thickness like plaster! I smiled and lifted my chin. "Mix that!"

She shook her head, opened the drawer to retrieve two more chopsticks, her 'handle' now four-kuaizi-thick. She didn't even need me to hold the bowl. Show off. And for some reason, the banana bread we made tasted better. I think the secret ingredient was effort. Yeah, yeah, and love.

Like us, children more appreciate accomplishments they put effort into. A little more effort, less electric energy used, family time, and an enjoyable end-result.

F. Grocery Store Coupons: Store coupons can save you lots of money if you use them to purchase food you'd normally buy, or they can cost you more money if you buy food items just because you have a coupon. But I suppose if you eat or use whatever it is you buy, you're good.

Double and triple coupon days are not as common, and too bad, 'cause man, they were great. My best pal and college roommate, John

G., and I, back in the day had this scam nailed to the highest header. We knew the cashier, Dawn, and she allowed us to use coupons against our charge even if we didn't buy the item. If the store carried the products, Dawn accepted the coupons. John and I could go in and buy a cart of groceries and walk out cash to the good. Beer money.

Once married, my wife and I clipped, filed, and made a conscious effort at using those little squares of waxy paper before the expiration dates. We saved a lot of bucks. Wine money.

Costco has great coupon weeks, savings of $2, $3, and $4 on selected food items, sometimes more than $50 on higher priced merchandise, like power washers. Bailey's Irish Cream money.

G. Entertainment Books: These things are awesome. The oftentimes very thick coupon books cover Sports to Spas, Restaurants to Recreation, Groceries to Golf, Movies to Maid Service, and Flights to Fandango Lessons. Yes, I know you have two left feet when it comes to fandango lessons but going out to only two 'two-fer' dinners normally more than pays for the cost of the book, around $35. (This may have been sometime back). And buying the book puts money in the till for a school club or organization, the Girl or Boy Scouts of America, MADD—Mothers Against Drunk Drivers, or DAMM—Drunks Against Mad Mothers. *My Dad was a card carrying DAMM member.*

I don't own a cell phone. Lisha just informed me that there are apps for coupons. Well, I'll be hornswoggled, there ya go.

Using two-fers exposes you to new and unusual restaurants, many of them Asian, and most you'd never normally venture into. But after hitting a few of these places, not only do you pick up on some of the language, but when friends ask if you've ever eaten cat or dog, you can answer, 'Maybe'. Chinese Food Syndrome from mono-sodium glutamate? No strong evidence to prove this, and MSG tastes great, one of my favorite seasonings. Especially with cat.

But let me warn you, using a coupon book can become addictive, compulsive, and *the* determining factor on where to dine. Not that this is a bad thing for us guys who use them since that is why we bought the dang things in the first place, but your significant other may take issue. For some reason—and I need to be gender specific here—women sometimes see men's habitual use of two-fer coupons when dinning out, as a disrespectful or thoughtless snub to how we men feel about *dem dar women.* If we really loved our current mate, we'd throw our wallets' health and well-being to the wind, buy the most expensive wine and order lobster since it is the highest price piece of fish on the menu. *Yes, I know lobster is not a fish! Just go with me on this.*

Women are too often impressed with guys who use valet parking, wear shoes that don't squeak, don't lace, and are made of some extinct lizard, and the silk-clad slick bartender who knows the spendthrift by his frat nickname, 'Hello, Biff'.

Fellas, if a woman judges you by your shoes or how you throw the keys to the too-inflated-tip-expecting wise-ass kid parking your car..., well, you deserve her. And she deserves you. Please don't have children.

My brother coupon clippers, stick to your guns. You will know that the woman you are with truly wants to be with you and may just appreciate your frugality. You can put the woman's priorities to the test if you pick her up in your three-year-old divorce mobile, a Chevy GEO perhaps, for that first date. If she says, "Oh, I hear these things get great gas mileage", she's a keeper. If she asks, "Is your regular car in the shop?", answer yes, and that you really own and drive a vintage Cobra, then never call her again after your Denny's dinner date.

Again, the warning, some women may take the issue to the extreme, breaking up with us and our beloved entertainment books that are kept accessible in our Geos. Tears will be shed, frustrations vented, sweatshirts returned, and toothbrushes thrown away. But fellas, look at the money you'll save with a hiatus on dating and dinners out, despite the two-fers. Singlehood is the ultimate less-expensive lifestyle. Yes, this *is* the voice of experience.

You can always opt to have meals out with buddies, just make sure you go out with two pals, not just one. If women see two men dinning together, females assume the men are gay—not that there's anything wrong with that. But it can certainly dampen the chances of meeting women while you are dinning out with a 'boyfriend'. I know this because it was told to me by women.

H. Doubling by Halving Amounts: When Kelsey and Jake were young, we drank a lot of juice. It didn't take me long to figure a way to stretch the shelf life. As I poured their cups, I added water to top them off. Topping off made for half the amount, a thinner apple or orange juice, but not a big flavor difference. Once the original bottle or jug was half empty, I'd refill it with water, and then we'd finish it off. The closest my children came to complaining was asking, "Dad, what are you doing that for?"

"Well, juice and water are both good for you, right? So, I'm making you a mixed drink. Good, huh?"

Do the same thing with bottles of Gatorade. Half empty one into the empty bottle of another, then top both bottles off with water. I still get the hydration and electrolytes I need on yardwork days and one case becomes two, an instant savings of about $20. Do this and you just paid for this book. I don't care if purple gets mixed with green, or red with blue to make green. When my workmates at Costco noted the strange colors and ask what I was drinking, I'd shrug and say, "I'm not sure." No, I do not do this with beer or wine.

I practice halving the amount of spread I put on sandwiches, as well as cheese slices. I use tea bags two-three times, add additional ice cubes to drinks, and my favorite is to add water to the coffee maker to run through the previous day's grounds. While living in China, I'd add hot water from my little electric kettle to my half empty cup of coffee, exactly doubling my amounts and exactly halving my coffee expense. "Well...", you say. "I'm not going to scrimp on flavor or quality." Need I remind you of the wine tasters? Okay, there is a taste difference, but my home has been paid off since 2005. Halving the coffee helped me do that. Really. Because it is a practice with so many other things, it does add up to considerable amounts of money to be better spent. *Full strength drinks, or no mortgage? Not a tough choice for me. And a habit I do not want to break.*

Add in the number of chunky children we see out in public who might be better off with half a slice a cheese on a minimally mayo'd sandwich of brown bread. And with no expensive candy in their lunch bag. How about a sweet apple, dried prunes or apricots or plums from your tree instead? No plum tree? Plant one, have your chubby kid work the shovel.

I'm again amazed at the number of very young children who recognize the packaging and wrappers of candy. They can't yet read, but scream out the brand names. Parents have allowed and encouraged this addiction. And then buy the candy again to shut the kid up. Yep, good parenting. And we wonder why youth become so easily enamored with drugs, pregnant, or fail in school.

I. Make Your Own Lunches: This doesn't take long, you chose to eat healthier, and you don't have to wait in line to buy expensive food. "Oh, but Mike, I don't have time in the morning to make my lunch or the kids'. It's so much easier for us to buy."

Well, you're not making time in the morning, and who says the lunches can't be made the night before? And when my kids got old enough, seven and nine, they were put in charge of making their own lunches, selections determined by me. Of course, they might ask to buy lunch on a day the school might serve a favorite of theirs. They had their own money—earned from me. Fine, their choice with their money. This helped to teach them the value of their earnings.

"That's unreasonable! You are such a jerk!"

Oh, yea? Let's give each of our young children $100 and see which kid spends it and which saves most of it. Then let's look to the future and see which of our now adult children max out their credit cards and are forever in debt and have no appreciation for being thrifty. I'll lay big odds. *I'd be cheating given both of my now grown kids have good jobs, own their own homes, and have money in the bank.* I rest my case.

And yet again, this is teaching children responsibility, self-reliance, cooking skills, food prep and safe food handling, and time management. But I'm a jerk?

"Well, that's just too young for kids to be doing those kinds of things."

Since when? My grandfather was plowing the family fields behind a horse and plow at twelve-years-old. I began mowing our yard with a reel push mower when I was six. I'm certain young kids can be taught to make their own sandwiches. As well as do dusting of the house furniture, run the vacuum, wash dishes, weed the yard, and a myriad of other chores they earn an allowance for. Kids are capable, and many enjoy demonstrating they are more grownup by assuming responsibility.

A young man I worked with at Costco was tens of thousands of dollars in debt. "Josh, you complain about having no money and being in debt, and there you sit eating a Costco hot dog." *I really liked this kid, we had excellent rapport, so I felt free to get on his ass about this spending habit. I was ready for his rationalization.*

"Ah, Moe, this was only $5."

"You do this every day?"

"Well, yeah. Sometimes pizza. I'm not spending that much."

"Well, you actually have less than not much if you are in that kind of debt, Dumb-ass. Let's say that you spend a *minimum* of $5 each shift. Five times a week equals $25. Four weeks in a month, $100. Twelve months in a year, $1,200. So right, not much?"

"Uh, I never thought of it like that."

"I'm here for you, Buddy."

Of course, I lead by example. My metal lunch box is known by all, made by L. May MFG, Sudbury, On. It looks more like a toolbox or a weapon. It easily holds my diluted bottle of Gatorade, the celery and carrot sticks I cut and sometimes peel, the boiled potatoes I never peel, my sandwich, an apple—I eat all but the stem, no surprise— some chunks of cheese, and a banana. I've always packed my lunch, and a nosy chubby teacher I worked with would look over my shoulder in the break room and observe—more like announce— "God, O'Neal, you eat like a goat."

"Yeah, but like some, I don't have a weight problem." *No, I didn't really say that. But wanted to.*

Chapter 2: CONSERVATION

A. Toothpaste: Halve the amount of toothpaste you put on your toothbrush. In fact, the electric toothbrushes some of you use are bristled in a circle smaller than the size of a dime. The action of brushing cleans your teeth more than the amount of toothpaste you use, Goof. I say that affectionately. Electric toothbrushes, way too expensive for me.

And squeeze that tub dry. If you take this to the next level, you can always slice open the expended tube with an Exacta blade to dig out the last brush-full of paste stuck at the top of the lid and along the inner sides of the tube. I must confess that even I don't do this, but I have used pliers to really pressure out that last dollop.

B. Nose Blowing: Use an article of clothing from the dirty laundry; a towel, shirt, or anything else that suits you. Morning nose blows normally take place in the bathroom where the hamper is anyway. Laundry day will take care of this, no problem. Gross, you say? What about blowing your nose into a hankie, pulling it out and reusing it, continually stuffing it into your back pocket where you repeatedly sit on it throughout the day? Or it goes back into a woman's purse next to their lip balm. Yes, if you are out and about, hankies do come in handy, unless you are practiced and proficient with the 'farmer blow'. You've seen this method used in movies like *Deliverance*. You plug one nostril with thumb or index finger and then blow a fast gush of air from the open nostril. I strongly suggest lots of practice before doing this in front of anyone, and not a good idea to do anytime before the fourth date.

While helping me do yard work, my young son failed miserably at his first attempt with the farmer blow, but it was hilarious! A pilgrim at this technique, like Jake, ofttimes soils not only their own shirt, but don't clear the tip of the nose, upper lip, and chin as well. Too much?

The tissue you might use at home can be thrown into the box or bag where you keep the old newspapers and junk mailings for starting your wood stove fires. This makes for less trashcan fill. Reuse.

C. Candles: Increase the life of big pretty candles by placing smaller candles or tea candles inside the melted hollow. This can be done a few times. When you have nothing left but a big cylinder of wax, use chunks of it to help start your outside fire pit fires. It's more fun and safer to watch the wax melt and ignite the wood than shooting much more expensive lighter fluid or even more expensive and dangerous white gas into your dwindling flames. How do I know not to splash white gas on a poorly lit fire? Don't ask. Let's just say I went without pruning my nose hairs and eyebrows for two weeks one summer.

D. Light Bulbs and Electricity: Just because a fixture has a three light bulb receptacle doesn't mean you need to use three light bulbs. Two, or even one, could do the trick. And as our parents have trained us, turn them off if you don't need the light or leave the room. Children take the cake with forgetting to hit the off switch. My kids learned at an early age to turn lights off when I began to charge them a quarter for leaving on an unneeded light. I might have collected a total of one dollar from each of them before they incorporated the good habit. Consistency with expectations and consequences is key to raising and training children. But note that frequently clicking lights on and off greatly diminishes the life of the bulb.

Anyway, if your overhead fixture has a cover, especially the one over your toilet, hiding that the 2nd or 3rd light bulb is not there, why not do that? How much light do you need to go poop? And when lightbulbs do burn out, they make a great BB gun target.

There's also this thing called 'Vampire Power'. Cool name. This refers to the energy sucked up by appliances just by being plugged in. Microwave ovens and televisions are notorious for still using energy while off, but still plugged in. Electric toothbrushes also a hungry Nosferatu in that category. I unplug things that are convenient to unplug, like my toaster, coffee pot, dancing *Caddy Shack* gopher. TV and microwave? Nah, too lazy for that, and the outlet is not easily accessible.

But Americans spend $3 billion a year giving electrical blood to the strigoi! If a power company were clever, they'd call themselves *Barnabus Power & Electric.*

E. Trash Bags: They are convenient, but unnecessary. Use plastic or paper grocery bags. This decreases the likelihood of smelly garbage since you are getting rid of the smaller bags much quicker. No big if you need to make more trips taking the garbage out. That's what your children are for, and if kids are unavailable or nonexistent, it's a little more exercise for you, and you probably need it. Even if you don't use any kind of bag, your kitchen trash can is most likely small and can be washed out and cleaned easily enough…, by your children.

If you must buy the drawstring bags, at least fill them up. "But if I throw chicken skin in the garbage, it will stink before the bag gets full." Okay, let me hold your hand through this one: Any wet trash that will stink quickly, throw into a grocery plastic bag, and toss it in the outside can right away. I realize that may have been tough to figure out, and it will require a few more steps in your day. I have faith in you. You can do it.

And lots of 'wet' garbage like vegetable peelings and other organic stuff can be given to the chickens. No chickens. A dog. Oh, you're a city slicker, no compost or earthworm box either. That's too bad. In the garbage it goes, I guess.

Unless your employer has a dumpster. Cancel your trash and recycle service and use your employers'. Of course, ask them first if this would be okay, careful to minimize the amount you might use it for, reminding them that they get a credit for the recycle which should make up for your discards. If they say no, just arrive earlier in the morning when no one will see you surreptitiously throw your grocery bag size of garbage into the bin. Remember to remove any identifying labels that could be traced back to you.

A custodian at one of the schools I worked for used the address labels as a trash owner search method to identify dumping culprits. I wouldn't have gone to the trouble, but Custodian Bob was on a mission. We were friends, so my trash was not a problem. We just kept it on the QT. I haven't paid for a one-can-a-month trash service for over twelve years now, amounting to a savings of over $5,000! It does add up, fellas.

These days I don't currently have regular access to any dumpster. But neighbor Tim is single, creating little trash on a weekly basis. The same goes for Lisha and I.

"Hey, Tim, here's a pumpkin bread Lisha and I just pulled from the oven. By the way, would you mind if I threw our trash into your half empty trash can once every two weeks or so? Nice. Thankyou. And I'll split wood for you."

Over the past few years, Tim and I have established a symbiotic relationship. Since neither household create much garbage or recycle, one waste can, and one recycle bin between us does the trick. Tim takes care of that. In return, I split his firewood. In appreciation for my hard work, he leaves a beer for me at the woodpile and gives us eggs from his nine-hen coop. In gratitude for the eggs, when Lisha and I bake, Tim is entitled to a loaf, a batch, or a plateful. Because he likes our cooking so much, he'll give us zucchinis from his garden for zucchini breads.

I love the good-neighbor cyclic barter system.

F. Tupperware: Use Tupperware rather than buy Zip Locks. In fact, no need to buy Tupperware. Wash and reuse emptied plastic tubs from cottage cheese, margarine, salsa, or whatever else might come in the sturdy reusable bowls instead of using food wraps and baggies. The bigger plastic tubs can be used for liquid cleansers when you do house jobs, or for pet water and food dishes, or for wood stain projects.

Empty bread bags and the likes can be cut in half and used as two or three baggies. I first saw another teacher doing this in 1984. I've done it since, sometimes reusing the same sandwich or carrot or cheese baggie for days.

Another wrap that can be reused is foil. I don't use a lot of foil, but it is good, sturdy stuff, can be cleaned and reused, and it is so completely recyclable. A three pack from Costco can last me a decade.

Lisha and I keep two old plastic containers near our sink. One is for the vegetable wastes we walk over to Neighbor Tim's chickens every two days—and we'll steal a few eggs—and one is for coffee grounds, good for plants. The grounds contain a helpful amount of acid, along with iron, calcium, and potassium, especially good for jade plants and roses. *We have permission to take eggs if Tim gets a homemade zucchini bread or chunk of Surprise Carrot Bundt Cake every now and then.*

G. Laundry: You don't need to launder your bath towel after each use. Hopefully, you washed yourself clean before drying off. Hang the towel up to dry and when it begins to smell too much like you, only *then* toss it into the dirty clothes to be used as a Kleenex until laundry day. And as you carry it to the laundry room swipe it along your bathroom counters or linoleum floors for a quick dusting. It's all about ergonomics, my friend.

Kids are notorious for two extremes: wearing the same favorite shirt, repeatedly without it being laundered, or wearing several changes of clothing in a single day, tossing what they wore while texting for twenty minutes right into the laundry basket.

Smell them—the kids and the clothes—and teach them about saving water. And wash full loads. On sunny days hang them—the clothing, not your kids—outside to dry. Yes, it takes more time, and some clothing can become stiff, but again, think of your children helping you do this while the sun is warm on your neck, the birds are singing, and the smell of cut grass is in the air. Clothes lines can't be used many days in Seattle, even in July. We Seattleites are more likely to hang them out for the washing phase. In fact, washing my truck while it's raining works out well, Mother Nature taking care of the wetting and the rinse cycles.

My brother and I used to chase each other under the drying sheets that draped two or three clotheslines, creating a tunnel, the smell of the detergent and bleach pleasant. Touching the clean sheets with dirty hands or knocking clothes pens away from my dad's frayed tighty-whities meant a sentence of five lashes with a peach branch. We were careful, pretending the clothing to be acidic if they touched our skin. Not such a stretch when it came to my dad's underwear.

Since we did not own a dryer for years, Mom would continue to hang the laundry well into the colder weather, our socks and underwear eventually pulled off the line semi-dry and frozen stiff. When the weather finally forced drying to the inside, the clothes were hung on a wooden collapsible drying rack that was unfolded over our gas floor furnace. These are some pleasant and nostalgic memories from an earlier era, and gawd, have I gotten old. I can't remember the last time I even saw a clothesline strung in a backyard in this country, let alone draped up over a floor furnace.

But all the apartments I lived in while in China had small porch sunrooms for hanging clothing, a recoiling clothesline fixed to the wall.

H. Dishwasher: Don't use one. Don't buy one! It is not much of a convenience anyway since you damn near need to wash the dishes before putting them in, then take time to load, unload, and dry besides. The noisy contraptions use lots more water than a filled sink and an abusive amount of electrical energy. By handwashing there'd also be a savings on dishwasher detergent, dishwasher repair, and dishwasher replacement, which becomes all too common with the things. You can wash, the kids can dry and put away, and again, you end up with a few minutes of conversation with your children.

If you've spent a day working in the yard—digging in the dirt, splitting wood— wash the dishes when you come in from those outside duties. The dish soap and scrub sponge are great for cleaning your hands as you do the dishes.

Done!

And make the conversations with you kids fun. Do not ask your kids about their failing grades, their goofy friendships, or their questionable attire. Ask them what their favorite frick'n color is. Their favorite movie and why; who their heroes are and why; do they think the world will be a better place 100 years from now, or a worse place, and why. What should be the drinking age in this country? How old do they think they'll live to be? Why are butterflies more valued than moths? Who is their funniest friend? What made them laugh the hardest that day at school?

You'll blow them away with questions and conversations like this and the answers you get might pleasantly surprise you. Or scare you to the point of hosting an intervention for your teenager.

The kitchen sink must face the yard, no matter front or back. If you are moving into a new home or apartment, this would be a must. If no outside facing window, cut one. If you live in a home where the kitchen is not walled and windowed facing a yard, sell and move.

Besides seeing the bobcat cross my driveway my yard is daily visited by deer, chip monks, squirrels, and all kinds of birds. And with my frequent viewings I'm rarely surprised by human approach, seeing the FedEx guy several steps before he gets to the door. I stop singing when I see him or her pull in.

I'm sorry if you live in a big city, but if your window faces the street, you might witness a car wreck, a mugging, or during the time of covid, an old Asian man being pushed to the ground. If you have a good trajectory, throw a can of vegetable waste at the attacker. Better yet, keep a brick at the ready on your windowsill. Recruit your neighbors to do the same! Neighborhood Watch would take on an entirely new meaning.

Finally, let me remind you how long clean dishes can sit in the dishwasher while dirty dishes pile up. C'mon folks. The children can do chores. Our homegrown Civil War, along with the 13th, 14th and 15th Amendments ended slavery in this country, but we do own our children, and we can legally have them earn their keep. If they accuse you of child abuse, lock them in a closet and slide pancakes and liver under the door for a few days. *I worry that some of you might think this a pretty good idea.*

H1. Garbage Disposal: Another convenience that uses power, can clog, short out, chew up silverware (or your kid's fingers!) and can break down. Set a fair-sized plastic tub near your sink for food scraps, peelings, and the likes. Yes, I've written about this already. When you like, walk the tub over to your Neighbor Tim's chicken pen and toss in the carrot peelings and apple cores. You might see the bobcat, perched and contemplating a chicken lunch.

Oh, yea, no neighbor with chickens. Throw the decomposable waste in your compost bin, use it for garden fertilizer in your garden or herb half-barrel.

Oh, right, a city slicker in an apartment; no garden area or half-barrel for growing herbs. Add some water to the tub, lid it, let it sit for a few days, take the lid off and dump it in front of a disliked neighbors' front door.

I. Heating & Cooling: Much of this depends on where in the world you live, so for simplicity's sake, I'll just address generalities. Basically, turn the central heating way down or off. Wear sweaters inside, cook meals on the stove for added warmth to your home, and fire up the wood stove, if you have one, and keep it burning 24/7. Cord wood cost way less than electricity. Don't you just love the smell of a wood fire? And the cozy ambiance. Watching the dancing flames is sometimes better than TV, depending on your reflective or romantic mood. Splitting and stacking your own wood, of course, warms you twice, saves you more money

Do not mistake my advocating of a wood stove for that of a fireplace. A wood stove will heat a room, an area, or an entire house depending on the square footage of your residence. There are some excellent wood stoves on the market that are very efficient at toasting a home, and the smell of a wood fire is one of the best aromas I know. Along with the exercise of cutting, splitting and the stacking of the cord wood—saving on a gym membership—takes the beneficial levels for good health and energy costs savings off the chart.   A question my Doc asks on each annual checkup is if I exercise. "Yep. Almost every day I work chores in my yard and split wood."

A fireplace is nice to use for that special date or added ambiance during the holidays, but because fireplaces draw air into them, the only place you'll feel the warmth is directly in front of hearth. Most of the house will get colder.

Gas fireplaces burn clean and are very convenient if you are willing to pay the price of the natural gas, which ain't the bargain it used to be when compared to using electricity. With a blower, they can heat some of the rest of home well, and they will also work if the power goes out. A family I knew stayed in a hotel for two days when their power went out because the inside of their home got too cold. They had a gas fireplace they thought wouldn't operate without electricity. Oops.

The top of a wood stove can also serve as a stove top. Storms will sometimes knock the power out for days in my log home. I crank up my wood stove. It soothingly casts both light and heat. I'll make up a pot of my prison stew and cook it atop my Lopi Liberty, then slurp my concoction by candlelight. Cooking this way is historically nostalgic, very satisfying, and the food more delicious for some reason. Sometimes very romantic, depending on the dates' view of roughing it. On windy stormy days Lisha makes sure her techno devices are pre-charged.

The quiet and darkness transports me back in time making it easy for me to imagine how my great grandfather must have ended his workdays on their farm in South Dakota once the ten kids were in bed.

One more thing, as you use paper products such as Kleenex, the rare paper towel, cardboard toilet paper cores, and obsolete note reminders, establish some type of scrap paper catch-all near your wood stove—a wooden wine box, an antique crock, a brass antique coal bin—for fire-starting. As well as being reused, it further diminishes your trash.

For cooling, wear less, open windows, use fans, prepare cold meat dishes like tuna salads for dinner, or set your cooling at a higher but still comfortable temperature. It befuddles (fun word) me how people will set their thermostats at 74 during the winter, but then at 62 in the summer. My average monthly power bill year-round is $35. My record low was $8! You do the math on savings.

With the hikes over the years in power costs, teachers I've worked with were paying over $700/month through the winter months. The coziness of wearing a sweater would seem worth it.

J. Gasoline: Americans are historically, socially, psychologically, and overall, characteristically: Stubborn, aggressive, self-centered, jingoistic, egotistic, strong—both physically and mentally—patriotic, oppositional, anal, caring, green-thinking, and ultimately independent. These characteristics are not good matches and ironic when it comes to conserving gasoline.

Since Hank Ford rolled out that first Model T on October 1, 1908, Americans very quickly became accustomed to the open road, going where they wanted to go when they wanted to go there, and doing so in privacy. They no longer had to wait for Dad to hitch up the horse so the entire family could ride into town for a $25 shopping spree of necessities. The advent of autos gave the horses a break from work and hauling young folks around on a joy rides and hayrides. Songs changed from *Tennessee Stud* to *Little Deuce Coupe*, and young men no longer had to sneak off with the neighbor's daughter to the too-near proximity of barn or alfalfa field for some quick romance. The auto became a bedroom on wheels and America saw a population boom in the 1930's. Go figure.

Not much has changed in that respect. Someone should do a study to figure the percentage increase of teen pregnancies that occurred in back seats of Buicks or the beds of Ford trucks for each decade beginning in 1930 to say, oh, I don't know, 2020.

But I'm getting slightly off track, pardon my booster seat.

Americans see the sense, and need, for rapid transit systems, metro buses, carpooling, and more economically gas efficient and electric cars. I have not had to argue this point with anyone. But—and this is me included—people do not want to give up the independence of driving their own vehicles, as well as driving the vehicle they prefer, and in some cases, this might be a gas-guzzling truck, a larger-than-life suburban assault vehicle, or the autos vindictive ex-wives buy using ludicrous divorce settlements to purchase Hummers or BMW's. (No, this did not happen to me, but it did happen to a friend of mine. Yes, he kinda deserved it.)

So, let's get back to saving dough, despite what you drive. Far be it from me to advise you to buy a Smart car that can also double as a coffin if you hit a squirrel.

Cut double, triple and quadruple lane corners. While driving, when you see a curve coming up, straighten the road and move to the inside lane, like a track athlete or auto racer who moves to the inside. If you do this every time, think of the miles you will save over years, whether on long trips or on your everyday commute. Besides that, it keeps me entertained and more awake on long trips. I'm very careful to not cut anyone off. "But isn't cutting across multiple lanes illegal?" Yea, whatever. Just check your rearview mirror for Chippies.

With parking, why is it so danged important for you to get as close to the entrance as possible? You end up driving the parking lot for minutes in search of the elusive front row slot. Park quickly, take a short walk. Again, walking is good for you. I purposely go for the rear lot spots, near the entrance/exit, knowing I'll find one, along with less fear of a no-looking person backing into me. As with all I am sharing with you it becomes a matter of adding up the little consistencies of your everyday life that will save you gas, time, and money.

In this same frame of mind, take your foot off the gas and let your auto coast down inclines and hills—if there are hills where you live, or while driving in the mountains—and if you drive a standard transmission, slap it into neutral. Over some mountain passes, like Siskiyou pass in southern Oregon, I have coasted for miles, getting up to over 70 mph, fun stuff in a Geo. Cops don't notice Geos.

Chinese drivers in Chinese cities make it a habit of putting their cars into neutral or into park at stop lights and in heavy stop-and-go traffic. Not that they know or care much about the Titan carbon footprint they are leaving, but they are very concerned with saving Yuan at the pump. When it comes to being tight, the Chinese have the Scots beat from Edinburgh to Llanfairpwllgwyngyllgogeryychwyrndrobwllllantysiliogogogoch.

I kid you not, that is the name of a railroad stop small town in Scotland. Been there, got the 2008 touristy visa stamp in my passport book to prove it. The name means St. Mary's Church in the Hollow of the White Hazel Near the Rapid Whirlpool and the Church of St. Tysilio with the Red Cave. Depending on the teller of the tale, the name was created by either a cobbler or tailor to bring in tourists since it would be the longest name of any town in the world. It worked. The tiny towns' shoppes do a thriving business during the tourist season selling everything from stuffed animals to hot plate slate stones with the name of the town appearing on the item. I bought the hot plate made of slate. Otherwise, how did you think I'd know how to spell Llanfairpwllgwyngyllgogeryychwyrndrob-wllantysiliogogogoch?

K. Dental Floss: I am shaking my head as I write this one. There is a couple —in a town I will not mention for fear of defaming the entire state—who *share* their dental floss. They claim it saves them hundreds of dollars a year. First of all, bullshit! My dentist hands out dental floss for free with each 4-6-month cleaning. (See below, THINGS YOU NEVER NEED BUY, 'H') But as fellow frugalists, the couple deserved mentioning.

L. Band-Aids: Too many times band-aids are applied needlessly, more for decoration or to mollify a whiny, cry-baby kid. As a teacher I was continually flabbergasted by the number of students, in their teens, who would ask for a bandage to cover a scratch or 'wound' I could barely see.

"You're not bleeding. Go back to your seat and pretend to be a little bit tough," I'd laugh. Who had raised these sissies? *Students can come up with the inanest of things to waste a few seconds of class time.*

My daughter and son helped me do yard work almost every other weekend when they were with me as young children, and then helped with building our log home just as they'd reached their teens. "Mike, the kids don't like staying at your house on the weekends," my lovely x-wife informed me over the phone one pleasant day. Or was I being scolded?

"Well of course they don't. I wouldn't want to stay with me either. Because over the weekend, we work. As you know, it is very important to me that Kelsey and Jake learn a work ethic. They get breaks every other weekend at your house where they sleep-in and play video games. It's different out here with me, a good mix, I think, between our respective homes." I probably didn't really say all that. My more normal response might have been more along the lines of, "So what?"

But I did say, "Do they also tell you that they get paid (*a whopping $5 a week*), we have nice dinners together, and after the dishes are done, we have popcorn and movie night?"

A counselor once told my ex and I, after we'd divorced, that our children did indeed have the good of both worlds in many ways. It should be no surprise to any parent that how our children turn out as individuals has much to do with the modeling behaviors they are exposed to. Thank gawd my ex-wife was patient, kind, forgiving, and nurturing.

Back to the band-aids.

While working in the yard one day, six-year-old Jake came up from his wood gather, interrupting my shovel work. "What's up, Pard?"

"Daddy, I got a owie. Can I get a band-aid?" He held up his dirty little hand showing me a scratch on a finger that was lined with blood.

I held out both of my hands, looking them over. "I've got three", showing him a popped blister and two bloody scrapes.

Little Jake appraised my small wounds, the popped and peeled blister he thought was 'cool' when I explained what it was. The look on his face was all too clear: The challenge was on! He forgot all about wanting a band-aid and *ran* back to his task. I laughed and forgot about it until the end of our workday when Jake approached me as we came in to get cleaned up.

"Dad! How many?"

"How many what, buddy?"

"How many owies do you have?"

I held out my hands and we counted five separate nicks, cuts, and blisters.

"Dang-it!", Jake said frustrated. "I only have four." From that point on I can't remember him ever asking for a band-aid. In fact, he told me years later, "Hell, Dad, a scab is a band-aid." I'd created a tougher guy. Way better that than a whiner.

Side story: Friends were over for a chicken dinner one evening. Kelsey and Jake cleared the table and began doing the dishes while we adults sat and visited.

Kathy leaned forward, asking, "Mike, when did you tell the kids to do the dishes?"

"I didn't. It's one of their chores and they just know to do it." It took Kathy and Steve several moments before their jaws were restored to closed positions.

Several years later, I got an email from my son while I was in Sharjah, teaching the spoiled brats of Sheiks of the United Arab Emirates. Boy, talk about not having a work ethic! Too many of these boys were as worthless as chickenshit on a pump house handles, but that's another story.

The email from Jake, read: "Dad, I just want you to know that there isn't a day goes by that I don't appreciate you teaching me how to work. Don't get me wrong, I didn't like all the chores I had to do as a kid, but my bosses here at Goggle see me as a rock star and really appreciate how hard I work. I owe it to you, Pops."

What better thing could a father read from their own child? My daughter conveyed it to me in another way. She and I were running errands one day in my truck when Kelsey got a call from a co-worker. At the time, Kelsey was an assistant manager at a sandwich shop.

"Tell me again why you can't make it to work. You stayed out late partying? Then you are quite the dumbass. You knew you had to work this morning, so what you did was pretty f-ing stupid. You'd better be to work on time, and you'd better work well. Otherwise, stay home, and when you feel better, look for another job."

Kelsey disconnected, expelling an exasperated gush of breath.

I grinned with pride. I advise raising children who scoff bandages.

M. Toilet Usage/Saving Water: You knew this one was coming. First on the list of water conservation is toilet-flushing. Growing up in Central California through the 1960's, 70s' and 80's, we had many alternating years of droughts and water shortages. Everyone knew the sing-song phrase, "If it's yellow let it mellow; if it's brown flush it down". Our household was respectful off that, besides putting a brick in our toilet tank to displace water. Later, when people figured out that bricks would slowly dissolve and potentially screw up the plumbing, a bright individual came up with plastic bags we'd fill with water and hang in the tank for the same purpose. These bags came to us in the mail in the early 1970's.

My girlfriend is from China. The Chinese have traditionally practiced conservation and frugality since before America was America. Once moved in, Lisha quickly and easily got me into saving even more water with showering and sink use by collecting it as it ran. We've placed buckets on the shower floors and big, but shallow, plastic bowls in the sinks. As the bowls and buckets fill, we use them to flush the toilets. One does need to aim the water as directly as one can to hit the hole in the toilet with the volume of the pour. Trickling it into the toilet won't work. You need to pour it with a quick fast dump. The toilet will flush. Think of the fun your younger kids will have with this one. The challenge? Get that floater down the chute!

She recently told me of Granny Sun, a neighbor who had become like a member of her family. Granny Sun tied, with string and rubber bands, her sink water handles, thereby allowing only a trickle of water to run. And the operator would need hold the handle to keep it running. "It was a pain washing dishes for her without a strong flow for rinsing, but we'd never correct Granny Sun's lifestyle in her own home. She had lived through some very tough times. We understood." I asked Lisha if Granny Sun was single. "Yes. Her husband died of thirst."

For homes that are not hooked up to the city sewer, like mine, then and now, we were in constant worry of our septic tanks causing us explosive, over-flowing, odorous problems. This made us much more conservative than the average bear when it came to over-use and frivolous flushing. As a kid growing up in the country, and now on the property of my log home, male visitors have learned to pick out a tree or to slip behind the shed to shake dew off the lily. Most men prefer this to going inside to use the toilet on bar-be-cue evenings anyway.

Another thing that really extends the life of a septic system and prolongs pumping by years is not flushing paper. I know this may sound gross to many, but primarily just to Americans. Many countries' (even if they have sewage services) systems can't handle the less soluble amounts of solid waste. People toss used paper into trash receptacles. The only Americans, who may practice this, own mountain cabins. This rule was evidenced by the following poem that was taped to the inside of the bathroom door, facing the toilet. My friends own a little place on Camano Island.

All we people with septic tanks,
Give to you our heartfelt thanks,
For putting nothing in the pot,

That will not absolutely rot.
Kleenex is bad, matchsticks too,
Cigarette butts a definite, non-degradable taboo.
No hair combings, use the basket,
There is a darn good reason that we ask it.
For you gals facing the monthly curse,
Wrap and trash the absorbent wick,
For better, or for worse.
So, in short, there's only two things to flush—
Your processed liquids and that will do…,
Oh, and of course, chewed and digested, #2!

My mother had a home in Havasu City, Arizona. Water service there is so expensive most people xeriscape front and backyards, using rock and cactus rather than grass. Smart. Even necessary. A leaking toilet or dripping faucet can add up to hundreds of dollars very quickly. The valley of Central California should xeriscape. As fertile as that valley is for agriculture, millions of cubic gallons of water are channeled in via aqueduct. The least homeowners could do, besides not flushing, would be to plant cacti and use hunks of granite instead of grass in their yards. Left alone, the valley would become a desert. Drive Hwy 43 towards the coastal range and check out the landscape if you doubt me. It is an alkali-ugly stretch of road, the landscape made up of sagebrush, loose loam, sand, pricky pear cactus, and coyote carcass roadkill.

Back to hand-washing dishes. Don't fill the sink with dishwater at the onset. Once the water runs to hot, begin washing, turning off the faucet as you wash. Nothing bugs me more than someone who lets the water run whether washing dishes, shaving, or cooling off hard-boiled eggs. Silverware goes into the washing sink first. *I'm assuming you have a side-by-side sink.* Forks and knives can soak. As you wash each cup or plate, run the hot rinse water over the cleaned dish into the washing sink. It'll fill up as you wash. I'd estimate you'd save a gallon or two of water easily with each pile of dishes washed.

And if not doing that many dishes, leave the water in the sink. It'll stay clean enough for the next time, even though it will cool.

And instead of running cold water down the sink while waiting for it to get hot, I run the hot to get it hot by filling my coffee pot, the watering can for plants, and the hot water kettle. The running water heats up without any going down the drain, and then I begin my dishwashing. Create procedure.

While living in the Mideast, and in Chengdu, China, I began the practice of shutting off the shower water while I soaped up. The water in both the buildings I lived in in both of those countries was stored in tanks on the roofs. There were many times the water did not heat up, and the tank could run dry on me. It became a simple matter of soaking myself quickly, turning off the water, shampooing and then washing my body with the shampoo suds, turning the water back on to rinse off. Done! *Okay, this did fail on me once. After I was soaped up, I turned the lever to only a last quirt of water before the tank went dry. I resorted to using water from the toilet tank. The water was a little rusty, but better a coating of rust than of soap. I guess. It made me look tan.*

I still practice this, using less than a gallon of water, half of which gets caught in the flushing bucket. Submarine boat captains would love me for the poster-child-navy-man on quick showers and conserving water.

Create conservative habits.

N. Razor Blades: To save blades or razors, and water, and soap, and time, grow a beard. But, for women in America, I'd draw the line with hairy legs and armpits. Sorry, I'm old fashioned and slightly too young to have been a hippy.

I use my disposable razors until they begin to pull out my facial hair or the plastic head breaks off from the hard tapping against the sink. My facial follicles don't grow in light, but I get over twenty shaves from one cheap disposable. And I don't use soap or shaving cream. Hot water does the trick just fine, my whiskers softened with the shower I've just taken. And I do not allow the water run. I rinse my blade in the sink catch-bowl.

And old razors remain sharp enough for shaving hairy cheese.

O. Ex-Girl Friends/Boy Friends: Don't burn bridges. Ex-lovers can be reused and are sometimes nice to reconnect with, especially if they are still good looking, are a decent cook, good at back rubs, fun, funny, and frisky. 'Nuff said.

And, other than a person who was abusive, why would you ever choose to lose touch with or be enemies with a person you once cared about? Ex-lovers are sometimes good for a second go, at least before you realize there was a reason you broke up with them—or they with you—in the first place. Recycling ('reusing' sounded too exploitive) an ex saves money on the first date impression thing and relaxes your time schedule while you continue the search for your unicorn.

Beware, each successive breakup becomes worse. My record was six and I almost didn't make it out alive.

P. Liquids: Always get that last drop. Put a little water in the ketchup bottle, swish it, and dump it into your next spaghetti sauce or prison stew. Salsa and hot sauce dregs, again slightly diluted with a bottle rinse can go into the next pot of beans or prison stew. Basically, determine what dish that remnant of flavor would match up with and add, easily done in—you guessed it—prison stews.

Dish soap. A little water in the 'empty' bottle can give you two more sink-loads of dishwashing. The same goes for liquid laundry soap.

When your coffee creamer bottle dribbles out, pour some hot coffee into the container, and swish it for your next cup. Plenty of vanilla creamer at the bottom and inside the bottle will mix with the added coffee for one more creamer'd cup o'joe.

Mayonnaise and mustard at the end, use a spatula.

Shampoo. Add water for 2-3 more shampoos.

Lay the 'empty' wine bottle on its side for a few seconds. It will create a considerable sip when poured one last time.

Balance your olive oil bottle upside down in pot or pan allowing the residual to drizzle and empty.

Again, all those last dribbles and drops add up when made a practice with all.

Q. Paper: We are so bad at wasting so much paper. I *love* trees to the point of being Druid. I've planted over one hundred trees on my property over the years. The kids and I bought living Christmas trees, then plant them the day after Christmas. Many of those trees are now close to one hundred feet tall, one a Giant Sequoia. It kills me to see so much paper and cardboard packaging misused, wasted, and tossed. It is completely recyclable, but even with our concerns for being 'Green' and the availability of recycle bins, we are still seriously remiss, disrespectful, and careless in the wanton manner with which we toss away our forests.

As a teacher, it drove me nuts to see other teachers push and harp on students to be 'custodians of the earth', when those same teachers ran multi-page worksheets using only one side of the paper. "Well, it's a hassle to run one side and then stack up the papers to re-run them through for printing of the other side". Lazy asses. *Not all printers at all schools have the big, fancy, expensive double-side printing printers. When I first began teaching, we still used Xerox machines—messy POS's.*

At the beginning of each year all teachers would be handed the updated version of the school handbook. Little would change from the previous year, amounting to maybe two or three pages of rewrites, but here'd come the 'new' 100-page binder for that year. And printed single-sided. Yes, I'd remind teachers and administrators of us being *Custodians of the Earth*, proper modeling to our students, and using the blank side of obsolete one-sided copies to run off new worksheets. I'd get polite, snarky nods from the old biddies, blank stares from administrators, maybe a 'Right on!', from the old hippie on staff, and that'd be the end of it.

Halfway through the year, after already plowing through our paper budget, the principal would suddenly and frantically announce that we needed to start conserving our paper and limit usage. "People, if you don't start watching the number of copies you run for your classes, we'll need to dip into the toilet paper fund to pay for copier paper. And we don't want that to happen, now do we? Ha, ha, ha." Fellas, that is a direct quote! Now it was my turn to give the snarky, eye-roll nod, followed by an extremely sarcastic, "Right oooonnnn!", then I'd stare blankly out the window.

At least some teachers passed their one-sided unused copies on to me. I kept a stack of it on a side desk as note and scratch paper for my students. I'd use the better sheets for the one-sided copies I needed to run. I rarely, if ever, ran copies on clean, unused paper. And yes, our district, like all others, would strongly support the next school levies. Hypocrites. The waste I witnessed in schools was extreme.

In more recent years it became a student requirement to bring a ream of paper to the homeroom teacher. I'd ask disgruntled parents if they paid taxes. "Of course!"

"Huh, you'd think the little bit of tax money needed for public education paper would be covered?"

"Hell, yes it should! I'm gonna talk to your principal!"

It was no wonder administrators kept a target-terminate-bullseye on my ass.

If you celebrate Christmas, birthdays, and other holidays with the giving of gifts, fold and save the once-used wrapping paper and set aside a bag for collecting the bows as gifts are unwrapped. The cost of wrapping paper is one of the biggest rip-offs there is. (Get it… rip off?) It is incredibly expensive, and the cardboard roll is thicker than the amount of paper on the roll! Newspaper is always a good alternative even though the Sunday comics are no longer commonly printed in color. When did that end? I hope it was for environmental reasons. More likely, stopping the comics section all-together, like with with some newspapers, saved the newspaper money.

Get clever with the headlines or advertisements in the paper. Exhibit that ad on the face of the package, be it political, an ad for hair loss cures, known faces in the media, or your own art on a paper shopping bag, another fun thing for younger children to do.

My resourceful Lisha has me in the habit of tearing a napkin in half for shared use. Why had I never thought of that one? I mean, how much paper does it really take to dab the corners of my mouth during a normal meal? And if that wiped blob of mustard wasn't too big, I leave my half of napkin on the table for my next meal. Next, I'll set it near the box of Kleenex for a nose blow. Lastly, I toss it into the waste-paper-collecting copper coal bin to help start the next fire in the wood stove. Finally, I use the stove ashes to fill low spots in my yard.

Sharing a napkin by tearing it in half, like the Gatorade, doubles your purchase.

I hope you guys are having fun with this read. Thank your wife or girlfriend again for getting this book for you. If you are not enjoying the read, use the pages as toilet paper.

R. Wash Your Own Vehicle: This is a very nice exercise to do on sunny days. Get a little bit of a tan, spray the kids or the significant other with the nozzle, laugh, run around the vehicle acting stupid—fun stuff. You know, just like in the movies. And save earthly water. Yep, I take it a step further. I wait until it rains. I leave my truck out the night of forecast rain. When the rain breaks during the next day, which it will likely do off and on throughout the day, I grab a rag, go out and wipe down my truck. Then I'll pull it in under cover, done deal. As much as it rains here in the Great Northwest, my truck stays relatively clean. And as much as it rains here in the Great Northwest, taking a car to the Big Bear Car Wash is a practice in futility.

"Dammit, I just washed my car and now it's raining."

"You live in Seattle, Dim Bulb!"

R1. Wiper Blades: I just learned a good buddy of mine may be even more frugal than me. He only replaces the wiper blade on the driver's side of his vehicles. Go Robert! His wife can't see out the passenger side, probably a good thing considering how Robert drives.

S. Stockpile: This can be considered if you've got the storage space. And you likely have the storage space if you've got a garage, a shed, space under your bed, a pantry, or an old car on your property. *I've always wanted a boxcar in my front yard.*

Many things don't rot or go bad, including assorted food items. Canned goods kept from the elements last for years. It's easy to tell if they have gone bad because the top of the can will bulge. If you're still not sure, when you puncture the lid, it will spit. If doubt remains, smell it. Or let your dog take a sniff. If the pup backs away, that's normally a reliably good sign. Other foods that last almost forever: Top Ramon, dry pasta, HONEY, dried beans, rice, most dried boxed goods, sugar, and Twinkies.

I recently found that flour goes bad. I discovered an old box of some instant dumpling mix. It contained the flour mixture for the dumplings and a can of chicken soup. What a rip-off. This was not anything I ever would have bought, but not sure where it came from. Anyway, Lisha's first bite told her the bread of the dumpling was sour. It took me three bites, but I did eventually agree. The next day I finished the soup but spooned out the dumplings into the chicken bucket. Lisha didn't even want me to pass the waste on to the chickens. The chickens did get sick, but I didn't. Neighbor Tim was mad at me. I wonder if we'll get any more eggs.

If a hard item is on sale, one that you know you will use down the road, buy it. It's on sale, and the next time around it sure won't be less expensive. I came across a good pair of urban hikers that were on sale some months back. Finding everyday shoes that I like is more of a challenge for me than I care to mess with. I liked this style, bought two pair. It's piece of mind for when the first pair wears out. *I hope I remember that I have the extra pair and where I put them. They say memory is the second thing to go when aging. Right, I don't remember what the first thing is.*

Over a year later I am still wearing the original pair, looking tattered, but the sole is still attached. Back in Costco, I saw the same brand, different style, on sale again. I bought another pair.

But two, get one free. I bought three cans, so got six cans of Planter's peanuts from Costco on two occasions. This is normally a good deal for food items, but can be attributed to other things like clothing, auto supplies, seasonal goods, and household sundries. Like going to a yard sale, if a shovel is marked at $1, why on earth would you not but it? I think I have four shovels. My favorite belonged to my grandfather. I keep them in strategic places under cover around my yard ready to grab.

And the tin peanut and coffee cans are perfect for nails, screws, paint brushes, and other smaller shed items, or toys, like marbles. Nothing like the sound of marbles being swirled in a tin can, eh?

Chapter 3: THINGS YOU RARELY, IF EVER, NEED BUY

A. Address labels. You sometimes get these for free from the American Heart Association, your alumni college, or your auto/life insurance agent, maybe from all the above. Who cares if your last name is spelled incorrectly by one letter? All the addressee cares about is the correctly spelled name on the check you've written enclosed in the envelope. A friend of mine gets so many address labels he finds the need to be rid of them. But then gets pissed at having to hand-shred them because the shredder would gum up due to the adhesive. I'd use them as tape to wrap gifts.

And if you happen to ever run out of labels, it takes an average of 17 seconds to write your return address in the top left corner of the envelope and in minimal amounts of ink from a pen you should have gotten for free from a hotel, bank, athletic club, or other business.

B. Paper towels: Use the dish rag, dish sponge or dish towel. A 'quicker picker upper'? Any hand towel is better, 'quicker', and more absorbent than a paper towel, and dish towels can be hung to dry. If you really must buy paper towels for what you perceive as a must-have convenience, a roll should last you two months if not more. And buy the paper towels that are serrated to tear into a smaller width. When done with them, into the catch-all for fire starting.

Right, with the COVID19 pandemic, paper towels became a way to keep that virus at bay as opposed to a multi-used rag or cloth. No argument. Why the hoarding of pandemic toilet paper? When asked by Costco members the reason for that, my answer was simple. "When people get scary news, they get the shits."

C. Shaving cream: All you need is hot water, sometimes not even that. You never saw *The Dirty Dozen*? All shaving creams are simply soap anyway. Ask Mr. Gillette. And don't let the water run while you shave!

D. Driving gloves: Are you kidding me?

E. Electric blankets: Just throw on another comforter or blanket, especially when considering a bed-wetter. Pissing the bed while the electric blanket is dialed in at level 8 could result in a shocking awakening. It'd be funny to see the morning hair, though.

F. Dryer sheets: What the hell do these things do anyway? And I have heard that the residue from the melting plastic can gum up the lint filter. Eliminate static cling? Static cling made folding clothes with my children lots of fun. We'd fold in the semidarkness of a bedroom to see the sparks, and the crackling noise of static electricity was the best! About once every two weeks, on laundry day, we'd have our own little waist level 4th of July. My kids would ask to help fold the clothes because of this. *I'm sure this had nothing to do with not buying toys for them to play with.*

I heard that if you stick a dryer sheet in your pants pocket or in your underwear that it keeps mosquitoes at bay. Fine. Buy the dang things, cut them in half, use one half for your dryer and the other half for a pocket in your hiking shorts. How do rumors like this begin? I also heard this doesn't really work; put it to the test if you like. If nothing else your underwear will be static free and maybe smell fresher as you walk.

G. Yard Art: Please, please, please, DON'T EVER buy Gnomes, wire and glass dragonflies or *any* 'decorative' patio bugs, plastic deer, plastic squirrels, plastic trees, plastic ANYTHING! Avoid plastic yard crap as if you'd receive the death penalty from Landscape Police! If you positively need a friggin' toy animal in your yard, sculpt it from wood, stack it in form from rocks, or weld it from iron.

On Interstate 5 between Central California and to the north of Seattle, side roads included, I have seen some pretty cool open-field and mountain-slope works of art made from scrap metal, painted on in situ talus or volcanic pushed up rocks, and hewn from fallen trees.

Flying dragons, snorting big-horned bulls, jumping salmon, udder heavy cows, menacing forest trolls, and a scaled down Noah's Ark to name a few of my favorites.

If your yard displays the plywood cutouts of those big-ended people bending over as if they are pulling weeds, consider yourself not even close to being affluent. No big deal, but why broadcast it? Call the police and have yourself arrested for crimes against humanity along the lines of Saddam Hussein after he torched the oil wells in Kuwait.

Ah, I'm only kidding. Those big-butted cutouts are kinda funny, money well-spent. *Actually, I'm just very afraid of Redneck retribution, so I just made nice-nice. And I can say Redneck because I've done field work.*

I do admire the larger-than-life, photo perfect painted farmers along the country roads and Highway 101 in and around Salinas, California. Cool, honorific, and classy. John Cerney does an amazing job with those 3D depictions, many of them a salute to real folk. They honor the hard-working farmers, store owners, police, and crop pickers in that valley—respectful tributes.

Other cooler-than-most things positioned in rural yards would be metal-rimmed tired tractors with their engines exposed and rusting to a lovely patina of rustic red. Any old farm equipment, old carriages and hay wagons, wagon wheels, gangster model round-bodied cars on bare rims but with windows unbroken, ship anchors and chain, rotting wooden dories on their sides, flower gardens planted within, and unpainted, unadorned boxcars, a kid's dream as a fort or playhouse. These are of the not-so-cheesy more rural works of yard art, rural the defining word. An old rusty tractor would not bode well in a Brentwood neighborhood.

Perhaps best of all, plant trees, shrubs, and perennials. Help to create oxygen, not eyesores, tetanus traps, or fungal spores.

And if you must line your driveway with old tires, don't paint them. At least some people find a use for the old tires, but I'd rather see them recycled as doormats or boot soles than as a rubber rainbow lining a driveway.

Since my grandfather was an Irishman, drank on occasion and wore thick glasses, his use for a single old tire was very clever. He hung it on the inside wall at the back of the garage as a bumper cushion for when he pulled in his new 1963 red and white Buick. Since I am related, I have done the same to the inside center ridge pole support log of my truck port. It serves as peace of mind for when I pull in in my new Ford F150 truck, especially after pub night. And I think of my grandfather each time. He died at eighty-three, but I didn't get near enough time with him. That tire serves more as a legacy and remembrance than a bumper bump.

H. Dental floss and STIM-U DENTs: Your hygienist should hand these items out, as well as a new toothbrush, after each checkup and cleaning or upon request. If your current dentist is too cheap to do this, fire the current, hire a newbie.

I. Christmas Cards: When compiling ideas for this little book, I was surprised at the number of my friends who wait until they get Christmas cards in order to resend them. Many original senders only note their family's name on the right inside cover under whatever greeting the card has printed within: 'Holiday Greetings', or 'May the Spirit of Christmas Bless Your Home', or my favorite is the one with Santa screaming at Rudolph crashed upon an outhouse, the card reading, "I said the Schmidt House!"

What you do is back-fold the card and tear off the decorative cover. You now have a single page Christmas card, blank on the backside. If it is close friends who sent the original card, send it back, wishing them a Merry Cmas and thanking them for the card. You may end up with extra cards sent by your insurance agent, dentist, the MDA, your Proctologist, and ex-lovers who want to recycle you, so rubber band them and save them for next year.

One of my friends and a friend of hers has sent the same card back and forth to each other for years now, a running tradition and joke between them. They cross out the previous year and write in the current with a renewed holiday greeting. Clever and fun.

My daughter is even more clever and funnier. If she gets an anniversary card, she'll resend that card to a friend who is having a birthday. The front of my last birthday card from Kelsey read, ***For the Girl Who Has Everything***"! Cracked me up. *You see, I'm not a girl.*

J. Cell Phones! I already know you are not going to give up your friggin' cell phone but hear me out anyway. I think you'll agree with me on many points.

Cell phones are expensive to purchase, although they are cheaper to operate than a landline. Granted. But how many cell phones do you own and how many times do you upgrade to the newer versions that have more applications than you'll ever use? Young people I worked with become so thrilled when they got the newest, more expensive versions of an iPhone or Android. These kids didn't make much money but would spend more than $700 on these things! And they told me $700 was a deal. $700 to me is a car payment. Hell, I *bought* a car for less than that once. *Of course, when I was their age my share of the rent in a townhouse, two-floored apartment was $67.50.* Right, your choice, and I'm told a necessity, but for me, why should I own one? Here's what I hear.

"Mike, you really should get a cell phone."

"Why?"

"So, I can reach you!"

"Call my home phone. I did upgrade to one that has a message recording deal."

"But what if I need to talk to you right then?"

"That might be your need, but not necessarily mine. And what on earth would you have done before cell phones?"

"But what if it's an emergency?"

"How many true emergencies do you have on a yearly basis, especially one that would involve me?"

"Well, you could think of others, you know?"

"I am thinking of others. As much as I dislike talking on the phone in the first place, I am saving friends and family from what would be my obvious impatience at being bothered. Heavy-assed sarcasm, snide retorts, and quite possibly verbal abuse that would shock a prison inmate could very well be forthcoming. And then I'd hang up on you."

"Well, what about directions?"

"I have maps in my truck, or I get directions before I leave." *Or, I admit, I rely on Lisha, who has her phone with her all the time.*

I hate it when I get together with people and the first thing that hits the table between us, even before the beer, is that miniature contraption of distraction and disrespect. During an entire evening of drinks and dinner, reflexive glances continually go down to that hard plastic and computer-chip-filled piece of crap, as if the owner is waiting to hear of an impending disaster or that the news has come through—they've finally won the *Publisher Clearing House Sweepstakes.*

I don't know about you, but I don't like it much when a call or text does come through, and I'm in the middle telling of one of my more entertaining tales or hilarious jokes, and the person across the table shows me the palm of their hand as a stop signal while they take their call. Motherfu... I went out with a woman who did that once to me. I went out with her..., once.

In the old days, an action like that would have been considered rude to the Nth. Oh wait, it is still rude! And cell phones give people an out if they are going to be late for a date or appointment, which makes them unreliable for ever being on time. "Aren't you supposed to meet Mike at 1:00?"

"Yeah, but I'll just call him on his cell phone and let him know I'll be a few hours late. Oh wait. He doesn't have a cell phone. I guess I'd better get going!"

I've had this confirmed by many. No, all! I ask if a cell phone lessens their concern for being on time. Every single person has answered in the affirmative. And recipients of the calls are too forgiving. "Oh, okay. See you when you get here." My rule is simple: You set a time you stick to it.

And people, especially of the younger generation, are not exercising or practicing memorization skills. That part of the brain, in this cell phone world, is atrophying. "What's your mom's phone number?"

"One."

"One?"

"Yea, she's my first person set to speed dial."

Well, that's just a busy signal of number 2! "What happens if your cell phone goes on the blink, you do indeed *need* to make a call to her and have to use another phone. If you don't memorize the ten correct digits, you could be up Cellular Shit Creek without an I-paddle."

"But, Mike, you can even talk into these things now to get directions, to ask it questions, and you can even say, 'Call So'n-so', and it's done!"

"Yes, and I can choose to read a map, write down directions that will truly take me along the correct route, and I prefer reading books than talking to a phone. Sure, it's Star Trekian fun (and complicated) technology, but I prefer a Daniel Boonian simplicity and not having such a reliance on batteries and electricity. Call me old fashioned. Because I am."

"Gawd, how did you ever get dates?"

"I visited the schools for the blind. I'd have tried *Match.com* but they charge a membership fee, and I would have had to spend too much time at my computer and too much money on first dates— meeting women who post twenty-year-old photos of themselves—for coffees."

"Did you ever look into foreign mail-order brides?"

"I would have, but most of them use cell phones and too many of them have learned to speak English."

Right, I'm never going talk you out of this one, but at least set that friggin' ear magnet aside and *unseen* when speaking in person with others, while eating, while having that all-too-little-time with your children, and especially while driving. Most states have finally gotten onboard with this one, even if drivers have not. My auto insurance man told me some time back that my rates continue to rise due to the number of accidents now occurring because of cell phones. "Mike, I used to deal with maybe one accident every two weeks or so. Now, it's more like two or three accidents a week!"

Back to my grandparents. They had no landline the entire time they lived in Thousand Oaks, California between 1936 and 1966. They used a pay phone down the road, deciding between parties when a family member call should take place maybe a month or so in advance. They survived and were happy, no ring-a-ling interruptions all day long.

K. Gifts: Admit it, you have re-gifted on occasion. Nothing wrong with that. Especially if you know that next person will enjoy the plastic gnome. Have an upper shelf set aside for unwanted gifts. Leave them in their original, unmolested packaging for that wedding you won't attend. If that next person doesn't want it, you've just given them a gift they won't have to buy when they re-re-gift it. Wouldn't it be apropos if you got that same present back in two years? It might become a contest as to how many years that gift makes the circuit, like that multi-used Christmas card.

L. Bar and Cain Oil: If you own and use a chainsaw, you've recently realized how much more expensive bar and chain oil has become. And if you own a chainsaw like my Poulan, it self-feeds, going through too much oil too quickly. Switch to vegetable or Canola oil. These natural oils work just as effectively and are obviously environmentally friendly as well as much less expensive.

Chapter 4: FREE STUFF!

A. Ink pens: From hotels, banks, athletic clubs, and assorted other businesses. Stock up. They'll be cheaper quality pens, but ink does not go bad. Oh, if your pen becomes clogged up due to disuse, hold a match to the tip. Yes, light the match first.

B. Hotel Soaps and Shampoos: Using the little samplers you can gather from hotels can serve as reminders of past trips every time you bath. If it is a bad reminder, pass it along to the x-lover you traveled with as a snub after you break up. A bag of these left on the door stoop can be perceived as thoughtful as well as snide, and therein lies the beauty of the dig. *Was he being thoughtful and nostalgic, or a jerk?*

Continuing to save on soap. Rather than trying to stomp and smear that last small disc into the shower drain screen, smash it onto the next bar of new soap. This equates to one, two, or more washings of an averaged sized body. I did a lot of traveling over a ten year period and collected so many little hotel soaps I didn't need buy bar soap for all those years and beyond.

In fact, there are many things you can take from hotels, guilt free. Along with the little soaps and small bottles of shampoos and conditioners there's toilet paper—a must-have-with-you, always, when traveling in foreign countries anyway—facial tissue, tea and coffee bags, miniature sewing kits, stationary, notepads, writing paper, pens again, envelops, and cardboard coasters. The one thing I advise leaving in the room would be the Gideon Bible: Bad karma if you steal a bible. I knew a man who once took one. He'd forgotten to bring a paperback along to read on connecting flights. He'd no sooner stepped from the hotel into the overcast of a Tokyo morning to catch a cab when from the 7th floor window came the splat of something on his head and down the back of his neck, the shot much to the envy of the local pigeons.

A child on the upper deck had run to the screen-less window to upchuck a load of too many mini bar snacks since mamma was busy and in the locked bathroom. The man reentered the hotel, paid for the use of another room to shower and clean himself up. He then surreptitiously returned the bible while the maid had the door to his previous room opened for her service.

Nah, I made all that up. But a good parable?

C. Socks: Airlines and medical exam offices offer these. Sure, they're thin, so use them as a first-layer sock along with woolen socks as a warm second layer in the wintertime or when hiking. Wearing two pairs of socks while backpacking and hiking will keep you from earning toe and foot blisters. On a recent visit to a doctor for an exam I'd rather not discuss, I got a pair of gray socks with cute little no-slip paw prints on the sole. Those socks are now my early-morning-weekend-coffee and writing-time socks. I have them on now, although I do not like recalling how I got them. When I think of the exam experience that earned them, more than one orifice of my body convulses and winks. I most definitely earned these cystourethroscoptic socks.

D. The Occasional Stamp: This is the stamp attached to the RSVP envelope for a wedding you'd never think of attending because you know the marriage won't last, or you have only been invited as an entity to increase the gift harvest. If you happen to later run into the mother of the bride, beg her forgiveness for not RSVP-ing, make your excuses and thank her for the stamp.

E. Kindling: Scrap wood is abundant if you keep an eye out for it. If you need junk wood to get your wood stove or campfires going, simply drive by construction sights. You'll be doing the contractor a favor by hauling away his splintered, end-cut junk wood that is piled up near the street to be scavenged. Check in with a lumber yard. They normally have a pile of it for the taking. Many times, behind grocery stores can be found broken pallets, some made of oak, which make for great bar-be-cue wood if you've got the Weber to handle it.

My Stepdad would saw the pallets into manageable pieces and strategically crib them in place in the half-barrel bar-be-cue grill he'd welded and made himself. Man, he cooked the best country ribs in that thing! He died a few years ago, and I still haven't found out who got that bar-be-cue.

F. Pallets: See 'E' above. I got many of mine for stacking my cord wood from the schools I worked for. The paper companies and other vendors who delivered on pallets were not concerned with getting them back, and my custodian buddy always let me know when the empty ones were left sitting outside on the loading dock ready for the garbage bin or for me. Some facilities will set their emptied pallets out roadside for the taking. When the pallets eventually break up and begin to deteriorate after years of holding my split wood, they become kindling.

Robert, of the single windshield wiper, has measured and cut pallets, making attractive country furniture from them; end tables— some with drawers—oak shelving, and an entertainment center. Amazing what a little creativity, a saw, some screws, and sandpaper can create. You'd never guess that these attractive pieces came from pallets.

G. Rebar: Staying along the construction side of things, rebar is another commodity that can be had in great quantity if one takes the time to network. I literally used a ton or more of this stuff in the foundation stem walls and in the pinning of my logs when building my log home.

A couple of my gym buddies worked construction. When I told them of my plans to build my cabin, they gladly offered their help, advice in the planning, and told me not buy rebar or plywood. At the time, Darryl was working a remodel job in the city and told me where to be with my truck on the day they were going to remove many ¾" sheets of plywood from a building roof. I was there at the appointed time. Darryl instructed the boom operator to lower the load alongside the bed of my truck. We slid the aged but still good sheets into the bed of my Ford. My truck got filled to tire-popping capacity. The thick plywood became my roof and sturdy sub-flooring, saving me a small fortune.

"Mike, I am working at two other sites. When we get done doing the foundation work, there will be piles of ½" rebar that the contractor will only end up burying instead of hauling it away. I'll let you know when you can come and get it."

Done deal. I got so much of the stuff that I was able to pass some of it off to other friends who were in need. I invested in a rebar cutter and bender I later traded for cement work on the foundation that became my master bathroom.

Recycling places also take in varying lengths of rebar. I've not been turned down when I make my request to scrounge for it.

H. Garage Sale Stuff: When you go to garage or estate sales, check out the shelves in the garage. Many times, there will be partially used cans of primers, paints, stains, and other toxic things that are regulated to not be dumped with regular trash. I took all the old stains from the wood shop class at one school, mixed them together, and the color exactly matched the stain of the logs of my home. It amounted to enough, enabling me to re-stain the front of my cabin to a nice reddish hue, close to the color of the natural hem-fir logs I built with.

If you are a 'Junker', you know way more than I do about digging out the deals at yard sales. The bottom line is that practice makes you good, and lots of the fun is learning as you go. A favorite line of mine is, "I'll buy this if you throw in that."

I. Look Down and Around: Along sidewalks, across school grounds, and certainly in store parking lots, keep your eyes on your feet. Besides the frequent coins and occasional dollar bills, people often drop Starbucks gift cards. Score!

I've also come across and picked up tools like new screwdrivers, a run-over but still functional measuring tape, a Chinese horse-tailed fly wand with a very prettily decorated hand-painted wooden handle, a monocular, rings, Apache arrowheads, a bag of Redhook souvenirs left in front of that brewery, a roll of postage stamps, a live box turtle, and reading glasses—pink, but they fit my ears and my magnification strength. The parking lots of Home Depots are great for finding things left in shopping carts. If you can't use or re-gift another measuring tape, take it back inside and get a store credit for it.

J. Notepads: Again, hotel rooms normally supply a scratchpad, name of the hotel at the top of each sheet, and when used back at home, hopefully a pleasant memory of a time away. Your junk mail offers up plenty of blank-sided half or quarter sheets. I keep the neat stack next to the kitchen phone.

Chapter 5: CLOTHING:

A. Kid's Clothing: Keeping-up-with-the-Joneses is a load of crap. Buying the name brand stuff amounts to purchasing an expensive label. If your kids want it that badly then they can chip in, work off the expense difference or otherwise earn it. Or maybe wait for Christmas, Chanukah, or Kwanza.

"But Mom, Johnny's/Susie's parents buy them this stuff. All parents do! I won't fit in! They'll make fun of me."

"Wow, they aren't very good friends if they make fun of your misfortune at having smarter parents who teach their children the value of a dollar, coping skills when dealing with bratty friends, and how not to follow the brainless spoiled Brat Pack. Those poor kids. They are destined to be drug abusers, teen parents, and still socially immature into their 30's. I'm so glad you won't turn out like that, Honey. Stores like Sears and J.C. Penny were invented for frugal, smart families like us. Try to keep from making fun of those so-called friends."

"Aren't both of those stores out of business?"

"That's beside the point, wise acre."

To spend a fortune on younger children's clothing when they will outgrow them in days is beyond silly. This is what older siblings and relatives, thrift stores, and school lost & found rooms are for. At the end of each school year, I'd ransack the lost & found closet for good— sometimes brand new—coats, sweatshirts, and gloves that were collected and in ample quantity. I even scored a great, brand new, wool-lined Levi jacket for myself back in 1994. I still have it, still wear it, almost 20 years later, the wear marks and one ripped pocket earned by me.

Second-hand thrift stores can be treasure troves of good clothing. Like-new items can be frequently found, play and work clothes abundant, entire racks of sport coats, sweaters, and nice dresses abound.

Good tools, dishes, antiques, books, and tons of household goodies take up large sections as well. A friend gifted me an old oak desk chair on working casters I've now been using for twenty-five years. I think it cost her $30. I saw a similar one in an antique store that had a $130 sticker on it.

B. Pre-Washed, Acid-Washed, or Pre-Ripped Jeans: Avoid. I could never figure why people would pay more for clothing that was already half worn-out, so would last half as long, just because that was the style. Growing up, we worked the wear and tear into our clothes, wearing them into style before it was the style, our favorite jeans lasting a year or more instead of only weeks.

And think of the poor cotton that gave its life only to have it diminished and squandered so thoughtlessly. It's 2022, and the rip thing is still in style. So, our affluent society wants to look poor? Growing up, my dad was embarrassed to wear holey clothes to school because he did not want to appear needy. Yes, America was a very different county in the 1930's. But it's too bad some of those conservative values have been totally tossed.

Chapter 6: THINGS TO REUSE BEFORE THROWING AWAY:

A. Wine Corks: A basket full of corks—especially if some of them are signed and dated—gives you bragging rights, and several of them can always be framed-in making hot dish plates (in the shape of a wine bottle), backing for memo tack boards, wine glass coasters (clever), or shaped into signs that read; MERLOT, or I'M A WINER. Or laid out and glued in the shape of a grape, a wine glass, or a fork = cork fork.

Yes, I realize crap like this shows a lack of maturity on my part. Your point?

My wife at the time laughed at me when I set out a basket full of wine corks that we had collected over five years at our garage sale. She wouldn't allow me to pack them up for our move to Washington state. "You actually think someone is going to buy those things?"

"Enh, it's worth a try. And if not, I'll give them to anyone who wants them for making tack boards, coasters, or clever signs that say, "Cork Off!" An old guy bought them for a buck.

I began collecting again, a habit revisited. Two friends have since asked for plastic bags full for their cork projects. I gladly handed them over, didn't even make a dent in my collection, I still had hundreds. If for nothing else, they can be used as kindling.

And then there was Lisha. "Honey, can I ask you a question?'

Uh-oh. "Sure, what…, my love?"

"Why do you have all those corks?" If men are half-smart, which I am, we learn to translate wife-speak. What Lisha was really saying—it wasn't a question—was, "Would you please get rid of these things." Just one day prior I'd taken the strong hint to recycle my stacks of empty peanut and coffee cans.

Gasp! Toss the corks? I couldn't. "I'll begin my hobo art with them tomorrow, my little love muffin."

In a couple of weeks, working leisurely, I created an assortment of cork trivets. It was so much fun. I was finally diving into those hundreds of corks that had been tossed into wicker baskets since 1991, and I was using scraps of saved lumber as well. A chop saw (miter saw) is one of my favorite tools to use, and I went at. I found an old jar of adhesive, I think originally used as a sealant, but it worked as glue for holding the corks in place. I found a small squeeze bottle of Elmer's Glue that was so gummy I needed to heat it in the microwave before it would flow. But I did use it first.

I was also able to use up some tiny nails that I'd found saved in a prescription bottle. Why I had saved them, no idea. Oh yea, I never throw anything out if it still has utility. But the best part was disassembling a rocker I'd gotten while in Costa Rica, 2002. New, it had been very nice; pretty, dark-stained wood, tooled burned scenes in the leather backing. It broke in 2012. I repaired it. It broke again, 2013. Into the shed it went. I just couldn't bring myself to turning it into kindling quite yet. And now, on my cork crusade, I could use both the wood and the leather from the rocker as framing and backing for my trivets of cork art.

A friend liked a big trivet I made from the rocker's curved base enough to hang it in their farmhouse kitchen. No, old tires don't line their driveway and they don't have garden gnomes guarding their radishes.

I used a wooden toilet seat for one that is now the base stand for a potted plant; yes, in the bathroom. My recent favorites are two small circular ones, the frames of which are two iron bands that held the rotting wooden hub tight of an old oak wagon wheel. As a kid I'd scavenged the complete wagon wheel from my grandfather's farm in 1968. I won't be giving either one of those coasters away.

B. Old Clothing: Discarded clothes should be passed on to the less fortunate if still in decent shape. The more raggedy become rags, and the outgrown go to the next smallest relative in line. When worn to the degree of a war refugee, old clothing can be used in pet bedding.

Old shirts are fun to use with dates who like having their clothing ripped off. Fellas, or gals, remember to cut a V into the neckline of t-shirts. T collars are hard to rent free, and guys, you don't want to look like you lack masculinity and strength if you can't pull apart the fabric. Plus, it's more fun to slowly rip from the top anyway. *Was that too much?*

Button down shirts for pirate ravaging purposes are lots of fun to abruptly pull open as well. A post-coitus game can be created for finding the sprung buttons. The round fasteners can fly off and roll to all corners of the room. You can make two coasters of buttons and corks when you have popped enough of them, then sign and date the coasters. Ahh, how romantic.

Old shoes should be stripped of their laces before being tossed, shoelaces making great ties for other things. When cut to shorter lengths they can be tied to zippers that are attached to backpacks, tents, luggage, and gym bags for an easier zipper grasp.

Mountain men whore buckskin shirts with laces of leather hanging off the arms and chest. Why? For repair. One could tell the length of time the frontiersman had spent in the wilderness by the lack of laces left on his shirt and pants. And when did tying a knot in a snapped shoestring end? I've worn laces that held three reties, or if the break occurs with enough lace left, I make-due with a shorter lace. Again, this was a practice learned from my depression-age dad. But as a real estate agent, not exactly a classy move when applied to his dress shoes. He tried to make sure his pant cuffs covered the fix.

My mom always swore that my dad's old tightie-whities made the best dust cloths. But my dad was so conservative having lived his early life during the Great Depression, that he would sometimes retrieve the underwear that my mom had 'graduated' to the ragbag. "Goddammit, these are still good."

As a kid I liberated a favorite pair of old Levis or a perfectly aged sweatshirt from the dog's bedding. "Mom! These are still good!"

Red clothing can be cut into strips, thrown behind the seat of any truck, and used for the mandatory daytime red flag if a load of board lumber hangs out past the tailgate of the truck by four feet—three feet in front if over the car or cab roof. I've used the same red shirt for years now. Why I ever had a bright red dress shirt in the first place, beyond me.

Old blue jeans can be stored for cutting up and patching other holey blue jeans. My wife at the time made a great backpacking canteen holder from a pocket of old Levis. I passed it back to her with some hotel soaps and shampoos when we divorced. A friend of mine is currently making a lap blanket of old Levis for me. *Christ, I've gotten old enough to warrant a lap blanket?*

Socks don't necessarily wear out evenly, the heal or toe blowing out of one but not the other. Set the odd one aside in the corner of your sock drawer in wait for the blow out of another one from another pair. Combine the two survivors. Right, they may not perfectly match, but if the colors match up at the ankle between shoe and pant leg, no one will notice.

C. Lumber: Do-it-yourself guys and carpenter hobbyist already known this one. We have an impossible time discarding that 8" long, 1"x 2" piece of cedar we might be able to use later. We lovingly stack it in our shed or garage. The spacing between garage wall studs is perfect for standing the longer, thinner boards and making them easily identifiable and accessible. If nothing else, we can lean over and smell the wood as we dick around in the garage or our shop. Ahh, the great aroma of pine and cedar. Trouble is, we end up with greatly varying sizes of white pine, yellow pine, knotty pine, Douglas fir, hem fir, red fir, maple, and oak stacked to the ceiling, three boards deep. Of course, we do occasionally use that stick or slab that we are now so glad we saved for seven years. Ahh, there it is! Just what I needed. But the unused pieces gather dust, mold, spider eggs and rat turds. This is when we might finally resort to cutting some of it up as kindling.

The deck I tore apart in 1999 from the rear of my manufactured home became the floor joists for my log home master bedroom in 2004. I nailed the decks 2"x 10" boards together, creating stronger 4"x10" joist, at no cost. My bedroom floor creaks—I should have used screws—but it serves as an early warning alert. It keeps vengeful ex-girlfriends from sneaking in on me at 3:00 a.m. and killing me in my sleep. That squeaky scavenged floor has thwarted three attempts.

The rough cut 4"x6" joists under my exposed deck began to rot after seventeen years, a good run. I pulled up the old deck boards, replaced the joists with married 2"x6"'s I'd set aside, and reinforced their bases and joints with several cinder blocks and old peer blocks that had been sitting in Neighbor Tim's yard for decades. I put all but three of the original deck boards back down. Does my 'replaced' deck look old and beat up? Yep. Is it solid? Very. But rather than costing me several hundred dollars or more, I did it for the price of screws and three new boards. My grandfathers would have approved and not thought to do it any other way.

The depth of my woodshed was determined by a stack of 2'x6's I got from a friend that I used as rafters. The awning was a stack of metal roofing I'd saved from years before, only slightly longer than the length of the rafter wood. The posts are trees from the back of my property. I dropped them, branched them, and cut them to size. Again, my only purchase; screws. And besides Lisha, I've got a few buddies who are more than willing to come out and help me. We drink beer, laugh, and I bar-be-que. The work is fun, satisfying, and ultimately far less expensive.

The same thing goes for nails, nuts, bolts, screws, pieces of wire, and pipe. If it still has the possibility for any kind of use, us guys simply *cannot* toss it, to the point of filling reused coffee cans with rusty bent nails. We can straighten them and use them in Oakie-rigged yard fix-it jobs. *I can say 'Oakie' because my grandparents were part of the migration west during the Great Depression in '34, only from South Dakota instead of Oklahoma.*

I am of the generation when the Cub Scouts *done learnt us* to make nut and bolt holders from baby food jars. The lids were screwed into a board that was in turn nailed to the bottom of a garage shelf. I think the one I made for my dad held five jars. He used them for washers, nuts, bolts, small nails, and screws. I was so proud that he was so proud of me for making that handy l'il catch-all.

If I haven't used the three to eight foot long 2' x 4's in two-five years, they go down on the ground as a base for my stacks of cord wood. After being on the ground for a year or two they begin to rot, then guess what? Correct! Kindling. As you have surmised, and I repeat myself, all these practices are basically a single practice of wasting almost nothing. The simple act of saving, reusing, and looking for deals is a habit I don't ever intend on breaking, regardless any wealth I may accumulate.

D. Wooden Chairs: When the leg of a wooden chair breaks, the right height bucket or log can be put in place of the leg for a perfectly good seat at the fire pit. If the chair breaks further while seated with friends around the fire, much to the hilarity of all, as long as you don't tumble into the fire, the chair can then be used as kindling for the next fire. If the same people come to the next cum-by-yah get-together, the story can be retold of how the chair had its final break for another round of laughter. *Mishaps make the best stories.* Right, with friends like this…. As a social rule of thumb, you should be the one who uses the rigged chair. No matter how good the friendships, there may be a pal not only as frugal as you, but of a more criminal mind who may be looking for a quick payoff through a litigation. On the other hand, the property owner protection insurance money could be split. *I do not suggest this, although a prison term would certainly lower your daily living expenses, medical costs, and grocery bills.* Need a costly surgery? Commit a crime that would incarcerate you for a spell.

E. Power Tools: Expensive. Hit yard sales. Get on the *Nextdoor* site. Buy two. Or have a talented friend reattach the cord that frayed and broke away from your power drill. Many parts of old tools can be scrounged and replaced, sharpened, and rewired. If the motor goes, no guilt with trashing it.

F. And…: Don't worry about small dings to an aging auto, furniture, or household goods. But yes, take care of your stuff. Good resell stories come from maintaining a pristine car or home. Better stories come from how that dent or hole got there. Yes, yes, fix up your home when it's time to sell. Get it looking so nice you'll not want to move, thereby saving a ton by staying there!

64

Chapter 7: MONEY

Searching the ground for coins is one thing, truly saving and spending money wisely, another.

A. Credit Cards: Ah, so convenient, and you can earn points, air miles, and credit/cash refunds. You save on postage stamps by keeping your card number on file with Amazon, your power and cable companies, and go paperless making for ease and instantaneous payments. Awesome! And after accruing a debt of hundreds or thousands of dollars, you only need make a minimal payment to stay in good graces, even have your credit limit extended. That is where the idiot part comes in.

Why on earth would you keep a balance in which you are charged an 18%, 19% or higher interest rate? Hell, even at an unheard-of rate of 10%, why would you want to pay that? If you are not making enough to pay it off, you shouldn't be using it. Continuing to buy is called ***spending beyond your means***. Overusing it has become a *bad* practice. You've given little attention or no consideration as to how much you've already charged on multiple credit cards for that month. Force some self-control over postponing immediate gratification. As Bob Newhart would say, "Just stop it!" I got my first credit card when I was twenty-one. What? I only needed to pay $35 for my month of charges. Cool. I think I did that twice before I realized the interest I was being charged. Screw that! From that time on, for well over forty years now, I have paid off my monthly debt each, and every single time, through thin and thick. Why on earth would I ever pay money for the privileged of using money, essentially buying air?

"But Mike, you need to establish and maintain a good credit rating, so you need to show a regular schedule of payments."

And who do you think started that rumor? Bullshit.

The only minor negative is that my credit card limit has ceased to be increased, but, oh yea, I don't need it increased because I don't take it to the limit. And my credit score? 830.

Over the years I have spoken to too many people who finally get this, but only because of financial woes. They become so excited when they are finally able to say, "Mike, after 83 years, I just finished paying off my credit cards!" Okay, maybe it was five years. Fellas, dammit! Willpower, postponing gratification, self-discipline, a budget, doing without doesn't necessarily equate to discomfort. Instill smart purchasing habits. Heard of any of this?

Another big payment you should desire to get rid of is your house payment—if you are fortunate enough to be buying a home. Granted, if you plan to sell your home to upgrade or relocate, this may not be such a big deal to you. But by knocking down your principal, you do increase your equity. I learned long ago that the years of a thirty-, or fifteen-year-loan can be halved by making one extra payment a year. The easiest way to do this is to add about $100 to each monthly house payment. I'd think that's manageable.

I'd allot for a certain amount of money to consistently exist in my checking account, the extra then added to my house payment, and it was sometimes considerably more than the minimum $100 I budgeted for. Any extra cash I acquired, same thing. To my mortgage it would go. I didn't piss the extra money away with frivolous spending just because it was surplus. My excitement came from a bigger balloon payment toward my mortgage.

I took out a new fifteen-year loan when I built my log home, most of that money going towards paying off the existing loan for the property. My goal: pay the remainder off in half the time; seven and half years. I did it in five years, and on a teacher's salary while sharing the raising of my children. How? See the pages above.

I tell ya boys, what a wonderful feeling it has been since then. Especially the part where that house payment amount now goes directly into my savings. That accrued amount enabled me to buy my last two Ford trucks, paying cash, so I eliminated a car payment as well. I've not needed to buy *anything* on time for a long time.

"But, Mike, you can't use your home as a tax write-off."

"Correct. The write-off amount would be nothing compared to

the total in interest costs I saved. I don't ever plan to sell my log home, but if I did, again the 100% equity. All mine, baby.

A property assessment lady showed up one day. After identifying herself, "I've got some bad news for you, Mr. O'Neal."

"Well, hello to you too." We laughed. "Break it to me gently."

"Your property value has decreased."

"Ha, that's good news! The value goes down, so do my taxes!"

"Gawd, Mr. O'Neal, I wish everyone saw it that way." Homeowners took out their perception of lost worth on her.

Side story: During the debacle of 2008, a friend stressed over her $80,000 depreciation of worth.

"You haven't lost or gained a dollar until you cash in your holdings. Sit on it, don't panic, wait this out." She couldn't do it. She sold off, thereby truly raping her account of $80,000. After reinvesting, she had regained her loses by 2017, but minus the $80K that would have been on top of that.

To potentially increase the sales of this book, the next few pages will be addressed to a broader audience. But fellas, keep reading. See if you agree with my encouragement and advice to the young.

College Students and Young Adults on Their Own

Lisha earned her second master's degree in International Development from George Washington University in Washington D.C. It didn't take her long to painfully discover how expensive living in the United States was, especially as a foreign student. *After spending just one year in China, my own culture shock was far worse upon my return to the US, hitting me smack dab in the wallet. $5 for a beer instead of 50 cents! Are you f-ing kidding me?* It didn't take Lisha long to find the school gave access to *The Pantry*. Panera, Target, and other stores, along with students who possessed abundances, donated to the campus store. Volunteers sorted and shelved the goods, mainly grocery items. Granted, Lisha got very tired of eating instant macaroni mixes, but she learned to get there early to score eggs, milk, fresh fruits and vegetables, and some frozen meats. Sundry items such as toilet paper, stationary, soaps, and kitchen utensils could also be had.

Robert, of windshield wiper fame, has a daughter who attended Cornell. That college had a reuse center called *The Closet*. Riley informed me that the rich kids who attended were generous with their donations of things other than food. Riley came across a nice tennis bracelet and other jewelry, board games, lots of school supplies and like-new clothing. She, like Lisha, took advantage of meetings, presentations, events, and seminars where food was made available. Not only did they get the one free meal they also snuck food out. Riley made a practice of grabbing a plastic to-go cup, filling it with food rather than drink, and walk it out. *Ha, not too far removed from the coal gathering of my grandfather.* I've no idea how many other colleges across the US offer such an opportunity. That would be up to you, the resourceful and intelligent student that you are, to find out.

The little faux stores on both campuses went without a monitor, and no one Lisha ever saw took an overload of goods. People in need are often among the most giving in terms of charity and being truly empathetic. For a few years running I took the lead in the school's seasonal food and gift drive for the Mental Health Association. I was meet with doubt and resistance from other teachers that first year.

"Uh, Mike, we're supposed to ask our students' families to give? Three-fourths of our student body live in government housing and have a tough enough time making as it is."

"Well, Ms. Negative Nancy, these kids and their families know what it's like to want. I can almost guarantee you that those kids and their families will give far more readily than our middle-class families who excuse their uncharitable thinking with, 'Hey, I earn a living, why can't they?', or 'If we handout handouts, they'll come to expect them!' But I'll tell you what, announce the drive to your students on Monday, and allow them to make the decision. How does that sound?"

Not only did the needier kids donate the most—hands down— they were also the ones who gladly volunteered, some with parents at their sides, to help sort, wrap, and distribute the donations. And the smiles on their faces broader than those of the recipients. Then there is the story of a not-so appreciative father of three.

The families' rental had been flooded out, destroying most of their furniture. Their church rallied, donating beds, a dining table, chairs, bookshelves, and more. Two of the kids were students of mine, the mother I knew from meetings and school events. In gaining that affiliation and rapport I was more than willing to offer my back and my truck to help gather donated furniture. Mark, another teacher, joined me. We met at their church at 10:00 a.m. on a Saturday.

Mom was on it. She had the route marked out so we wouldn't be back-tracking, which I really appreciated, also denoting what we'd pick up at each stop. I needed to know this so I could plot my tetras moves in how to load my truck and the POS trailer she was pulling behind her car.

"Great, you guys have fun." I thought the dad was joking. But he got in his car, drove away. I think my face contorted into three different expressions of disbelief and anger at once. I looked at Mom, my eyebrows deeply furrowed. "Oh, he's leaving his job, and they are throwing him a going-away party."

I nodded and got into my truck with Mark. "Are you fucking kidding me!?"

Mark tried calming me down, reminding me of why we were helping the family, but man was I ticked. The man of the house was off to drink punch and eat cake! What kind of a rat-bastard thinks like that? We worked most of the day driving from home to home and loading up, the three children pitching right in and taking directives well. In my late teens I'd worked for a furniture company making deliveries, so this was old hat to me. We filled my truck and the trailer twice, dropping the loads at the storage place.

Dad showed up, all smiles, at the storage unit when we were unloading the second and last load, mid-afternoon. "You guys done?"

How about a 'Thank you', ya worthless turd? "Yep. Did you bring us some cake from your party besides the crumbs on your shirt?"

"Yea, but I ate it on the way here, hahaha."

Mark put his hand on my shoulder, needing to Spock my trapezoid to keep me in place.

Sorry, back to being a needy college student. Gawd, I feel for you. Moving out, whether for college or to just get out and be on your own, is not near as financially easy as it used to be. Across the nation rents can be prohibitively expensive. I lived with three roommates because we wanted to cut our costs. As I related in an earlier section, we splurged on a townhouse, second and third floor roomier apartment, my share of the rent, $67.50. But this was in 1976; no cell phones, no internet, $2.00 movie tickets, fifty-nine cents a gallon for gas, and my monthly full-time wage was just over $600. But today's costs have far surpassed relative inflation and costs of living. The rental fees you young folks face almost make it a necessity to take on five roommates. You are one of the main reasons motivating me to write this little book.

And yet, as intelligent, respectful, and as nice as you young people are, I do not see you budgeting well. You so often deserve the title, 'entitled'. The Greatest Generation of the 1940' & 50's got married in their early 20's, bought a home, began their families, and may times never moved. My generation tried to buy, expected to stay in that home for a while, eventually trade up with new mortgages that would last forever. Then refinancing, taking out a second, sometimes a third loan, improving that home, and paying the bank back forever. It could take twenty to thirty years to settle on a home Baby Boomers would eventually call home.

You, this next generation does not expect to wait that long. Many of you think you should have what it took your parents years to gain, immediately upon becoming adults. For twenty years now I've seldom seen a young person driving a beater—a secondhand car. Your new cars are either bought for you by your parents or you suck it up and make big car payments for five years. Thus, you are in debt early in life. Maybe this is the crux: You get so used to debt, it's no big deal. Like my young friend at Costco, tens of thousands of dollars in debt, no plan or real concern for alleviating it.

Having taught and then work with younger people I am impressed for the most part. Most kids are well-spoken, of good humor, intelligent—not the same as wise—and have a decent work ethic. But I question the money sense of you great kids. You often complain about not making enough money, but then opt to be cut from the work schedule if given the opportunity on any given day. That's like a man dying of thirst in the desert but refusing offered water because it's not purified. A previous generation or two would have sipped on piss.

Making and bringing your own lunches is sporadic at best, and as I mentioned, your autos are newer and fancier than the ones of a generation ago. Granted, my generation spent a stupid amount of money fixing up our old cars: Mag wheels, stereo systems and 8-track tape decks, pen-striping, and split manifolds. But jazzing up our jalopies was far cheaper than buying a new car. There was also the added expense of speeding tickets. But let's get back to today's young people not budgeting and how goofy their spending is.

With Covid-19 came forced savings. Bar hoping is a very expensive activity, along with dating and going out. I'm sorry your social lives have been impeded, but think of the savings, maybe a good lesson to be learned. You've become creative with dating, a revisit to old-timey practices of private picnicking and those kinds of outings opposed to populated partying. Nice, isn't it? Your parents and grandparents are now cooler than you thought, eh? When social distancing finally ends, I hope you remember some of the fun and creative adjustments you've had to make.

Now roommates. Parents often advise not to room with your best friends, but who the hell else would you want as a roommate? Nonetheless, advice to be considered if not adhered to. The trick is to talk with and establish ground rules before any lease is ever signed, no matter how closes you *think* you are with your buds. Food purchases and consumption, lights out, dates and company curfews, study/quiet/bedtimes, respect for space and cleanliness, shared bills, especially with electrical use; heating and cooling, lights, appliance use, anything that has a plug should be discussed. Not many things are more frustrating than one roommate who keeps tabs on shutting off lights while another roommate sets the thermostat at 62 degrees during the summer, and 75 through the winter.

My first roommate experience was 50/50 deal. Well, more like 25/75. One roommate and I were on the same page, the other two or three, (our inhabitants varied from four to five guys, with an occasional short-term sixth thrown in) not so much so. In short, they were slobs. I'd gather up all the discarded and tossed clothing, dirty plates, cups, wrappers, and books, throw all into a big pile in the middle of the front room, thinking they'd get the hint. Nope. Each guy would dig through the pile, retrieving what they needed and move on. Then they were senseless enough to ask why a vein in my forehead was protruded and pulsing. They began to get the hint when I threw the entire pile over the balcony. My communication skills had much to be desired when I was nineteen. All of this does relate to money. These guys could be just as thoughtless when it came to sampling my groceries.

One roommate helped himself to my leftovers from a Mexican restaurant. My taste buds were all set for that remaining chili relleno. When I saw it was gone, I denounced the Alamo icons; 'those damned gringos!' Rather than homicide, I opted for sweet revenge. I waited three days before I struck.

"Mike, did you eat my pralines and cream ice cream?"

"Yes, I did. You ate my Mexican food."

"But you hate pralines and cream!"

"Yes, I do. But you love it, you bought it, so we're even. Revenge truly is best when served cold."

Roommates need to set some clear and precise rules and expectations, and those agreements need to be mutually and respectively adhered to. Certain expectations that one may consider as universal common sense and a simple matter of good manners may not even be a fleeting fart-of-a-thought in the other roommates tiny, knotted head. Young people, be wise to take nothing for granted, make no assumptions. And don't let things fester. Calmly and respectfully deal with all issues as the arise. Attack them in their sleep only after the second warning.

If the two, three, or four of you have similar tastes and eating habits, go ahead and purchase groceries collectively. But if one person in that mix eats like a recently released refugee on the run, the equal parts cash contribution may need to be adjusted, the food rationed, or resort to individual buying. And label your food or have individual designated areas of pantry and on fridge shelves.

Ya know, I just realized my audience. And since this isn't texting or another form of techno media, I'm probably losing you. So, let's make it simple:

Renter/Roommate Discussions for Rules and Agreement

- Agree on inside thermostat temperatures for summer and winter.
- Food: Collective buying, separate shelves or labeling to show ownership.
- Times for study, social, quiet, lights out.
- Common use of dishes, paper towels, toilet paper, Kleenex (dirty clothes), furniture, light bulbs, toothpaste, detergent, and other sundries.
- Dirty dishes! I strongly suggest this adage: 'you use it, you wash it, immediately.' No piling up of dishes.
- House cleaning and chores: Taking out the trash, dusting and keeping common areas clean—strongly suggest all pick up after themselves. Vacuuming, toilet flushing, bathroom and kitchen wipe downs, and is there any kind of yard space to care for? ***Clean as you go*** or a weekly cleaning schedule.

• No loaning of money, especially for rent. A roommate needs moola, they need to ask the parents who didn't teach them to budget. *An apartment neighbor of mine, Don, a nice guy, asked me for a loan of $20. I knew he already owed several other people. I laughed, told him no way. "Don, it is common knowledge you ask too many people for 'loans' and then don't pay them back.   I like you, think you're a good guy, but don't bother ever asking me for money. He never asked me again, and we remained friends.*

• No borrowing of clothing, car, hairbrush, girlfriend, sporting equipment.

• Television programs and volume. This was easy for us. The several roommates I had between 1976-1983 didn't own one. When my son got his own place, he bought one for himself, hung in his bedroom.

• Absolutely no illicit drug use! Unless you all use drugs. Then you deserve each other.

I had to give equal time, and to not leave out the younger kids. Have fun going over this with them, Dad!

Children, Coins, & Collecting!

Hello, kids! Money is cool, right? Coins are fun to collect, paper money is full of Historical information, and if you save enough money, you can buy presents and some things for you and your family.

First, do you know what money is worth? Money is all about math. Let's take a look. Take out some of your coins.

One penny. Abraham Lincoln is the man on the coin, our 16th President. He was president during which war, 1861-1865? The Civil War. This was a war over states' rights and slavery.

The penny is worth the smallest amount; 1 cent. Since copper has become more valuable, the penny is now made mostly of zinc. If your penny has wheat strands on the back (see picture), save it! They don't make those anymore.

The nickel. How many pennies does it take to equal a nickel? Since a nickel is worth 5 cents, yep, 5 pennies.

That's Thomas Jefferson on the coin.

Which President was he?

Does your mom or dad know?

Thomas Jefferson was our 3rd President. He wrote our Declaration of Independence. He loved gardening, playing the violin, building and inventing things, was tall and had red hair. If you knocked on his door, he might answer wearing a robe and slippers.

So, 5 pennies = 1 nickel.

Next is the dime, worth 10 cents. Franklin Delano Roosevelt is the man. Many people refer to him as FDR. He had polio.

FDR was the only President to be elected 4 times. Now, Presidents can only be elected twice. The 22nd Amendment made this a law in 1951. Easy to remember: 22nd Amendment, 2 terms.

Another easy one: A dime is worth 10 cents, so how many pennies make up a dime?

10 pennies = 10 cents = 1 dime.

And how many nickels make up a dime?

2 nickels = 10 cents = 1 dime. Very good!

Now the bigger coins. Which one is next?

The quarter. Why is it called a quarter? Just like on a measuring cup, one quarter is written ¼. So, what is a quarter ¼ of? If you know a quarter is worth 25 cents, does that give you a clue?

How many ¼ cups make up 1 full cup?

So, four ¼s = 4/4, = 1 full cup. Confusing?

Too bad. Dad, take over.

Just kidding. Maybe one of your parents is a math teacher, cook, or carpenter. Or maybe they graduated from 6th grade.

If a quarter is worth 25 cents, how many quarters make up $1? Add 25 cents 4 times, or multiply 25 x 4.

Correct. 100. 100 what? Correct again! 100 cents!

Okay, fill in the blanks!

_______ pennies = 1 quarter.

_______ nickels = 1 quarter.

It takes _______ dimes and ______ nickel to = 1 quarter.

George Washington, our 1st President, is the face on the quarter. Washington was the leading general of the troops during our Revolutionary War. That's the war in which the newly declared United States of America fought the British to gain Independence, 1775-1783.

He and Thomas Jefferson were friends.

The story of little boy George chopping down a cherry tree is not true, although many people believe this story. It's a fib about how you should tell the truth. Sometimes adults are weird.

Beginning in 1999, state quarters began to be minted. The reverse—the back of the coin—shows something notable, historical, or important for that state. Do you think you could collect all 50 state quarters? Yes, there are 50 states.

How many coins have we looked at so far?

Do you have a big piggy bank? How full is it?

Do you do chores around the house to earn more coins? Ask your mom or dad or grandparents or neighbors if you can do jobs for them to earn money. Rake, pull weeds, sweep decks, change the oil in the car?

What are you saving your money for? It's okay to save it and not spend it anytime soon. The more you save up, the better thing you can buy.

Do you have a savings account at the bank?

Only two more coins to go, and they are worth the most.

Next is the 50-cent piece. Let's do the math first! I like math, especially when adding up money. Again, fill in the blanks.

How many pennies is a 50-cent piece worth? _________

It takes _________ nickels to make 50 cents.

_________ dimes = 50 cents.

Just _________ quarters = 50 cents.

Do you recognize these men? On the right is Ben Franklin. He was never a President, but he knew George Washington and Thomas Jefferson. In fact, he helped Jefferson write the Declaration of Independence. Franklin loved learning and was good at doing many things. He is what we call a *Renaissance Man*, a guy who has an interest in many worthwhile activities.

He was an inventor.

He was a writer.

He was a very famous and popular statesman. A statesman is a person who loves the art of government and works for changes that will help others. At least that's what a politician is supposed to do.

He stayed fit by swimming.

And he was known for having a good sense of humor. I think you would have liked him. Your dad and I would liked to have had a beer with him.

He kept active and loved learning, and that's probably a big reason he lived to be 84!

At 83, he was the oldest member at the Constitutional Convention in 1787. The Constitution lays out the Law of our Land. If you want to become a lawyer, or care about the rights of Americans you'll need to learn and know the Constitution.

If you ever get a Franklin half dollar keep it. They stopped making them in 1963.

Instead of being worth 50 cents, collectors will pay more than $30 for one coin!

The other man is JFK, which stands for John Fitzgerald Kennedy.

He was not the youngest President. The youngest President was Teddy Roosevelt, at 42. Teddy was FDR's cousin.

Teddy was Vice President, becoming President when President William McKinley was shot and killed in 1901.

But Kennedy was our youngest *elected* President. He was 43. Kennedy is remembered for supporting the space program, beginning the Peace Corps, and choosing not to vacation in Cuba.

And now, $1 coins. $1 is worth 100 cents.

$1 coins used to be huge! See the two coins below.

The older silver dollars were called Morgan, and then Peace Dollars. Instead of being worth $1, these coins are now worth lots more! They can be worth $30, $50, or even more than $100!

The man on the newer silver dollar is Dwight D. Eisenhower. He was our 34th President, and before that he was a Five Star General. He was in both World War 1 and World War 11.

His silver dollars were minted from 1971-1978. They are also a good coin to collect snice they are no longer minted.

The newer dollar coins are much smaller. In fact, the Susan B. Anthony coin was unpopular because people often mistook them for quarters, and vending machines would take them as quarters.

These coins were only made 1979-1981, and then they were tried again in 1999.

Susan B. Anthony protested and fought for social changes in America. She was against slavery and wanted more rights for women.

She thought that women should have the right to vote.

Even though she fought for women's *suffrage* (voting) in the 1860's, women were still not allowed to vote in national elections until 1919, with the 19th Amendment; another easy association with the 19's.

Next came the Sacagawea gold coin in 2002. No, these coins are only the color of gold, not made of real gold. The baby on Sacagawea's back is her son Jean Baptiste Charbonneau.

Yes, Sacagawea helped Lewis and Clark on their two-year journey across what would become the United States, from sea to shining sea. Jean Baptiste was born during that trip.

The men kept their complaining quiet during the rough times since the baby did not whine or cry hardly at all. Sacagawea was strong, intelligent, and tough. Clark liked her so much he later let her two children live with him and he sent them to school.

In 2007, these coins began depicting (showing) the Presidents in order of their presidency. Four Presidents a year would have coins made with their faces.

See if you can collect all the different Presidential coins!

It's too bad you can't return pop bottles for money these days. That was how I started my coin collection. And when I worked for neighbors doing little jobs, they paid me with quarters and half dollars.

I chopped cotton for my grandfather when I was 12 years old. He paid me in half dollars. I never spent them.

I loved making and saving money. In the Fall, beginning when I was 5 years old, I'd go door-to-door in my neighborhood with a rake over my shoulder, and offer to rake leaves.

The trees on my street were Fruitless Mulberries, and they shed a lot of big leaves. Of course, my little brother and I jumped in the high deep piles we raked up.

As I got older, I took on more difficult outside jobs.

I mowed lawns, cut wood, pulled and dug out weeds, cleaned garages, swept sidewalks, and washed cars.

And my parents gave me an allowance for doing chores at home.

I put my money in my bank account, collected coins, and had a lot of cool piggy banks.

You are never too young to start saving money. And you are not too young to work and earn it.

Okay fellas, young and old and in between, if nothing else I hope you had fun while reading. If I stepped on any toes, well, they probably deserved at least a little treading upon.

I remind you of how truly wasteful and eco-unfriendly we remain as a nation, and I'll assume some of the guilt. I'll bet you've remanded my continued references to burning a wood stove for heat and enjoying my outside fire pit while sipping wine and communing with friends.

Guilty.

I'll leave it to you to come up with your own trade-offs, environmental as well as energy savings, as well as the emotional well-being gained from whatever makes you happy.

Not wasting money is the best way to save money.

And probably one of the best adages of all when deciding to purchase or not to purchase.

Do I really need this, or simply want it?

This has been fun. Take care, fellas.